MW01107981

LAYERS OF LEARNING
YEAR FOUR • UNIT NINE

TOTALITARIANISM
U.S. ECONOMICS
VOLCANOES
ABSTRACT ART

Published by HooDoo Publishing
United States of America
© 2017 Layers of Learning
(Grilled Cheese BTN Font) © Fontdiner - www.fontdiner.com
ISBN #978-1546841364

Units at a Glance: Topics For All Four Years of the Layers of Learning Program

1	History	Geography	Science	The Arts
1	Mesopotamia	Maps & Globes	Planets	Cave Paintings
2	Egypt	Map Keys	Stars	Egyptian Art
3	Europe	Global Grids	Earth & Moon	Crafts
4	Ancient Greece	Wonders	Satellites	Greek Art
5	Babylon	Mapping People	Humans in Space	Poetry
6	The Levant	Physical Earth	Laws of Motion	List Poems
7	Phoenicians	Oceans	Motion	Moral Stories
8	Assyrians	Deserts	Fluids	Rhythm
9	Persians	Arctic	Waves	Melody
10	Ancient China	Forests	Machines	Chinese Art
11	Early Japan	Mountains	States of Matter	Line & Shape
12	Arabia	Rivers & Lakes	Atoms	Color & Value
13	Ancient India	Grasslands	Elements	Texture & Form
14	Ancient Africa	Africa	Bonding	African Tales
15	First North Americans	North America	Salts	Creative Kids
16	Ancient South America	South America	Plants	South American Art
17	Celts	Europe	Flowering Plants	Jewelry
18	Roman Republic	Asia	Trees	Roman Art
19	Christianity	Australia & Oceania	Simple Plants	Instruments
20	Roman Empire	You Explore	Fungi	Composing Music

2	History	Geography	Science	The Arts
1	Byzantines	Turkey	Climate & Seasons	Byzantine Art
2	Barbarians	Ireland	Forecasting	Illumination
3	Islam	Arabian Peninsula	Clouds & Precipitation	Creative Kids
4	Vikings	Norway	Special Effects	Viking Art
5	Anglo Saxons	Britain	Wild Weather	King Arthur Tales
6	Charlemagne	France	Cells & DNA	Carolingian Art
7	Normans	Nigeria	Skeletons	Canterbury Tales
8	Feudal System	Germany	Muscles, Skin, Cardio	Gothic Art
9	Crusades	Balkans	Digestive & Senses	Religious Art
10	Burgundy, Venice, Spain	Switzerland	Nerves	Oil Paints
11	Wars of the Roses	Russia	Health	Minstrels & Plays
12	Eastern Europe	Hungary	Metals	Printmaking
13	African Kingdoms	Mali	Carbon Chemistry	Textiles
14	Asian Kingdoms	Southeast Asia	Non-metals	Vivid Language
15	Mongols	Caucasus	Gases	Fun With Poetry
16	Medieval China & Japan	China	Electricity	Asian Arts
17	Pacific Peoples	Micronesia	Circuits	Arts of the Islands
18	American Peoples	Canada	Technology	Indian Legends
19	The Renaissance	Italy	Magnetism	Renaissance Art I
20	Explorers	Caribbean Sea	Motors	Renaissance Art II

3	History	Geography	Science	The Arts
1	Age of Exploration	Argentina & Chile	Classification & Insects	Fairy Tales
2	The Ottoman Empire	Egypt & Libya	Reptiles & Amphibians	Poetry
3	Mogul Empire	Pakistan & Afghanistan	Fish	Mogul Arts
4	Reformation	Angola & Zambia	Birds	Reformation Art
5	Renaissance England	Tanzania & Kenya	Mammals & Primates	Shakespeare
6	Thirty Years' War	Spain	Sound	Baroque Music
7	The Dutch	Netherlands	Light & Optics	Baroque Art I
8	France	Indonesia	Bending Light	Baroque Art II
9	The Enlightenment	Korean Peninsula	Color	Art Journaling
10	Russia & Prussia	Central Asia	History of Science	Watercolors
11	Conquistadors	Baltic States	Igneous Rocks	Creative Kids
12	Settlers	Peru & Bolivia	Sedimentary Rocks	Native American Art
13	13 Colonies	Central America	Metamorphic Rocks	Settler Sayings
14	Slave Trade	Brazil	Gems & Minerals	Colonial Art
15	The South Pacific	Australasia	Fossils	Principles of Art
16	The British in India	India	Chemical Reactions	Classical Music
17	The Boston Tea Party	Japan	Reversible Reactions	Folk Music
18	Founding Fathers	Iran	Compounds & Solutions	Rococo
19	Declaring Independence	Samoa & Tonga	Oxidation & Reduction	Creative Crafts I
20	The American Revolution	South Africa	Acids & Bases	Creative Crafts II

4	History	Geography	Science	The Arts
1	American Government	USA	Heat & Temperature	Patriotic Music
2	Expanding Nation	Pacific States	Motors & Engines	Tall Tales
3	Industrial Revolution	U.S. Landscapes	Energy	Romantic Art I
4	Revolutions	Mountain West States	Energy Sources	Romantic Art II
5	Africa	U.S. Political Maps	Energy Conversion	Impressionism I
6	The West	Southwest States	Earth Structure	Impressionism II
7	Civil War	National Parks	Plate Tectonics	Post Impressionism
8	World War I	Plains States	Earthquakes	Expressionism
9	Totalitarianism	U.S. Economics	Volcanoes	Abstract Art
10	Great Depression	Heartland States	Mountain Building	Kinds of Art
11	World War II	Symbols & Landmarks	Chemistry of Air & Water	War Art
12	Modern East Asia	The South	Food Chemistry	Modern Art
13	India's Independence	People of America	Industry	Pop Art
14	Israel	Appalachian States	Chemistry of Farming	Modern Music
15	Cold War	U.S. Territories	Chemistry of Medicine	Free Verse
16	Vietnam War	Atlantic States	Food Chains	Photography
17	Latin America	New England States	Animal Groups	Latin American Art
18	Civil Rights	Home State Study I	Instincts	Theater & Film
19	Technology	Home State Study II	Habitats	Architecture
20	Terrorism	America in Review	Conservation	Creative Kids

Unit 4-9 Printable Pack

This unit includes printables at the end. To make life easier for you we also created digital printable packs for each unit. To retrieve your printable pack for Unit 4-9, please visit

www.layers-of-learning.com/digital-printable-packs/

Put the printable pack in your shopping cart and use this coupon code:

2317UNIT4-9

Your printable pack will be free.

Layers of Learning Introduction

This is part of a series of units in the Layers of Learning homeschool curriculum, including the subjects of history, geography, science, and the arts. Children from 1st through 12th can participate in the same curriculum at the same time - family school style.

The units are intended to be used in order as the basis of a complete curriculum (once you add in a systematic math, reading, and writing program). You begin with Year 1 Unit 1 no matter what ages your children are. Spend about 2 weeks on each unit. You pick and choose the activities within the unit that appeal to you and read the books from the book list that are available to you or find others on the same topic from your library. We highly recommend that you use the timeline in every history section as the backbone. Then flesh out your learning with reading and activities that highlight the topics you think are the most important.

Alternatively, you can use the units as activity ideas to supplement another curriculum in any order you wish. You can still use them with all ages of children at the same time.

When you've finished with Year One, move on to Year Two, Year Three, and Year Four. Then begin again with Year One and work your way through the years again. Now your children will be older, reading more involved books, and writing more in depth. When you have completed the sequence for the second time, you start again on it for the third and final time. If your student began with Layers of Learning in 1st grade and stayed with it all the way through she would go through the four year rotation three times, firmly cementing the information in her mind in ever increasing depth. At each level you should expect increasing amounts of outside reading and writing. High schoolers in particular should be reading extensively, and if possible, participating in discussion groups.

These icons will guide you in spotting activities and books that are appropriate for the age of child you are working with. But if you think an activity is too juvenile or too difficult for your kids, adjust accordingly. The icons are not there as rules, just guides.

☺ 1st-4th

☻ 5th-8th

☻ 9th-12th

Within each unit we share:

EXPLORATIONS, activities relating to the topic;
EXPERIMENTS, usually associated with science topics;
EXPEDITIONS, field trips;
EXPLANATIONS, teacher helps or educational philosophies.

In the sidebars we also include Additional Layers, Famous Folks, Fabulous Facts, On the Web, and other extra related topics that can take you off on tangents, exploring the world and your interests with a bit more freedom. The curriculum will always be there to pull you back on track when you're ready.

www.layers-of-learning.com/layers-of-learning-program

UNIT NINE

TOTALITARIANISM - U.S. ECONOMICS - VOLCANOES - ABSTRACT ART

I always consider the settlement of America with reverence and wonder, as the opening of a grand scene and design in Providence, for the illumination of the ignorant and the emancipation of the slavish part of mankind all over the earth.

–John Adams

LIBRARY LIST

HISTORY

Search for: Bolsheviks, communism, Stalin, Lenin, Hitler, Nazis, national socialism, Mussolini, Warren G. Harding, Calvin Coolidge, Franklin Delano Roosevelt, progressivism, socialism, Russian Revolution, 1920s

☺ 1920s Fashion by Emily Bone. A sticker paper doll book.

☺ American Family of the 1920s Paper Dolls by Tom Tierney.

☺ The Wonderful Wizard of Oz by L. Frank Baum. Read aloud to even younger kids.

☺ A History of US: Book 9: War Peace and all That Jazz by Joy Hakim.

☺ Stalin by Albert Marrin.

☺ Hitler by Albert Marrin.

☺ Angel on the Square by Gloria Whelan. Historical fiction set in revolutionary Russia.

☺ ☺ Animal Farm by George Orwell. This is a story of animals on a farm who revolted against the farmer. Before long the leaders of the revolt begin to treat some of the stupider or "lower" animals very poorly. The phrase "some are more equal than others" comes from this story. Must be discussed out loud.

☺ 1984 by George Orwell. Written in 1949, this was a futuristic dystopian novel in which the government goes to extremes in surveillance, informants, and thought control. It is a rough around the edges story, so if you're concerned, pre-read or read it with your teen. It delves into themes of freedom of speech and thought and the consequences of losing that. Use Spark Notes to help with discussion.

☺ The Origins of Totalitarianism by Hannah Arendt. A dense read, a classic, an effort worth your time. Avoid Benediction Books edition as it is full of errors.

☺ Mein Kampf by Adolf Hitler. Read it with an eye to comparing Hitler's worldview to what you see in politics today.

☺ The Road to Serfdom by F.A. Hayek. Explains the dangers of political philosophies we're very familiar with today.

☺ One Day in the Life of Ivan Denisovich by Alexander Solzhenitsyn. A fictionalized account, but written by a man who really did spend ten years in a Soviet Gulag. Political prisons are hallmarks of repressive states. This is what it's really like when you lose political freedom.

☺ 1920: the Year of the Six Presidents by David Pietrusza. A cross section of 1920 in America, especially the political side of life.

GEOGRAPHY	Search for: economics. Though all of the books below are children's picture books, use them for all ages. They teach economic concepts simply. Older kids will be able to apply the lessons to the real world and their experiences in it on a grown-up level. ☺ If You Buy A Mouse A Cookie by Laura Joffe Numeroff. Illustrates the concept of unlimited wants in a finite world. ☺ The Three Little Pigs by Paul Galdone. Use this to teach opportunity cost. ☺ Buy My Hats by Dave Horowitz. Demonstrates supply and demand. ☺ Alexander Who Used To Be Rich Last Sunday by Judith Viorst. Use this to teach kids about impulse control and saving. ☺ ☻ The Have A Good Day Cafe by Frances Park. Use this book to teach about competition. ☺ ☻ One Hen by Katie Smith Milway. Use this book to teach about entrepreneurship and how business owners benefit their communities. ☺ ☻ Ox Cart Man by Donald Hall. Teaches about goods and how selling them translates into buying what we want for ourselves. ☺ ☻ Henry's Freedom Box by Ellen Levine. In the story a boy toils in slavery while his greatest wealth, hard work and ingenuity, are stolen from him. Use this to talk about how the most important source of wealth a person has is his labor. ☺ ☻ Uncle Jed's Barbershop by Margaree King Mitchell. Use this to teach that a level playing field (i.e. without government discrimination) is necessary for capitalism to produce prosperity. Also discuss how to work for delayed rewards. ☺ ☻ Isabel's Car Wash by Sheila Blair. Teaches about how investors and entrepreneurs win when they take risks. Also explain the results if the venture were a failure.
SCIENCE	Search for: volcanoes, geysers, volcanology ☺ Volcanoes by Franklyn M. Branley. ☺ The Best Book of Volcanoes by Simon Adams. ☺ Eye Wonder: Volcano from DK. ☺ ☻ Volcanoes by Seymour Simon. ☺ Volcanoes & Earthquakes by Susanna van Rose. From DK. ☺ Volcano: A Visual Guide by Donna O'Meara. Full of full page, full color photographs of volcanoes with little blurbs of text that explain the structures. ☺ ☻ What's So Hot About Volcanoes? by Wendell Duffield.
THE ARTS	Search for: abstract art, Pablo Picasso, Georges Braque, Wassily Kandinsky, Jackson Pollock, Piet Mondrian ☺ The Noisy Paint Box: The Colors and Sounds of Kandinsky's Abstract Art by Barbara Rosenstock. A Caldecott Honor book. Highly recommended. ☺ ☻ What's the Big Idea: Activities and Adventures in Abstract Art by Joyce Raimondo. Step by step projects that teach the techniques of great abstract artists. ☺ ☻ ☻ Color Your Own Abstract Art Masterpieces by Muncie Hendler, from Dover. ☺ ☻ ☻ 13 Modern Artists Children Should Know by Brad Finger. Part of a series.

HISTORY: TOTALITARIANISM

Famous Folks

This is a self portrait of Boris Kustodiev.

He was a famous Russian artist. In the west he is most known for his over-sized "Bolshevik peasant leading the people in revolution," but most of his art was much more cheerful and shows an entirely different side of Russia.

This painting is called "Blue House" and was painted in 1920 as well.

Look up his art.

The 1920s and 1930s were times of economic prosperity and then economic disaster. They were also times of recovery and re-action from the horrors of World War I. There were both political and economic factors that led to the rise of totalitarian states.

The rise of 20th century totalitarianism started with the Bolshevik Party of Russia and the Revolution of 1917. The Bolshe-viks, and nearly every other totalitarian state (notable exceptions in the Middle East), were built on the ideas of Karl Marx. Marx thought that workers should seize power from their masters, fac-tory owners, and the nobility (see Unit 4-4 for more on Marx).

This painting by Boris Kustodiev was done in 1920. He named it "Bolshe-vik" after the political party that had led the people in revolution just a few months before.

Next, after World War I the Germans tried to rebuild their nation and institute a republic. Hampered by immense inter-national debts, the Germans made bad financial decisions, de-stroyed their economy, and paved the way for another socialist, Adolf Hitler. A similar story was playing out in Italy and Spain where both countries, groaning under financial troubles and bad government, turned to socialism to solve their problems.

In the United States outright socialism wasn't popular, part-ly because of American traditions of freedom and partly because America was wealthy. Even the working class of America was better off than many of the well-to-do of Europe. But America did suffer under poor financial decisions which led to the Great Depression.

In 1920 though, the future looked very bright. The war was over, women were gaining legal rights, business was booming, a new invention was coming out every other week, the real economic prosperity of everyday families was increasing year by year, and the whole world was becoming very modern.

☺ ☺ ☺ **EXPLORATION: Timeline**
Printable timeline squares can be found at the end of this unit. Use them on a wall or in a timeline book.

- October 1917 Bolshevik Revolution in Russia
- Aug 1918-Mar 1919 Post-war recession in the U.S.A.
- 1920 Bolsheviks have solidified their power and Russia is renamed Union of Soviet Socialist Republics (USSR)
- 1920 More Americans now live in towns and cities than on farms
- Jan 1920-July 1921 Severe recession hits the U.S.A./Europe
- Nov 1920 Warren G. Harding wins presidency by a landslide
- 1920-1933 Prohibition of alcohol in the U.S.A.
- 1923 German hyperinflation
- Aug 1923 Harding dies in office, is succeeded by Calvin Coolidge
- Jan 21, 1924 Vladimir Lenin dies, Joseph Stalin takes over
- Aug 1928 Kellogg-Briand Pact "outlaws" war
- Nov 1928 Herbert Hoover wins presidency
- 1929 One car for every four Americans is on the roads

☺ ☺ **EXPLORATION: Totalitarianism**
Totalitarianism means a government that has absolute control over its people. The government decides what the people read, watch, and do. It decides where people work and how much time off they have. It decides what people learn and even tries to control what people think and believe. In the twentieth century new types of totalitarian economic systems were tried, including communism, socialism, and fascism.

Some of the nations that became totalitarian were Russia, China, North Korea, Italy, Spain, Argentina, Chile, and Cuba. Find these places on a map of the world.

Some of the people who implemented controlling governments wanted to control people so that everyone could be equal; others just wanted to have power.

Think about what it would be like if parents could not decide what church to take their children to or if teachers and schools could not decide which textbooks to use. What if moms and dads could

Famous Folks

In the 1900s people started using words as propaganda. Calling the Bolshevik government a "republic," for example, is ridiculously inaccurate, but it kept Western reporters pacified and quiet for decades. Textbook writers and politicians are almost pathological in their misuse of terms, so be sure you double check the real intended meaning of the words being used in the books you read and in the speeches you listen to.

Additional Layer

There were several recessions between 1899 and 1930. All, except the Great Depression, were recovered from quickly and completely, emerging with stronger economies than before the recession. What was different about 1929? Read and find out.

Teaching Tip

Coming up in unit 4-18 we'll be discussing civil rights in depth, so for now it's okay to skim over topics like women's vote, the KKK, treatment of blacks, and workers' rights, even though they're so much a part of this time period.

Teaching Tip

We chose just four dictators to keep the Exploration manageable, but you can add more by finding images online and printing the faces.

We also chose dictators from different places in the world so that your kids would understand this was and is a worldwide problem, not confined to one culture.

Famous Folks

Benito Mussolini was a fascist dictator in Italy from 1922 to 1943. He invented fascism and was an ally and role model for Hitler.

Fabulous Fact

In the 1920s people first began to buy luxuries like ready made clothes, home appliances, automobiles, pre-packaged foods, radios, and movie tickets. These became commonplace for most Americans.

not decide where to work or how many children to have? What if kids were forced to join certain clubs and spy on their parents? What if instead of the police being there to make sure everyone followed the law, they were there to bully people? These are some of the things that happened in these countries. In some extreme cases the people who didn't agree with the government would disappear and be taken to work camps or killed, their families never knowing what happened to them.

Make a rotating stage for some dictators from this period. You will start with a cardboard box, gray spray paint, a small dowel, and the printable dictators from the end of this unit.

1. Cut out a rectangular space on two opposite sides of the cardboard box. Spray paint the box gray.
2. Decorate one side of the box to look like a fancy government building. The other side should look like a prison. On the government side write, "I wanted to . . ." and on the prison side write, "What happened was . . ."
3. Cut out the dictators, and cut a slit top and bottom so the dowel stick can slide through.
4. Cut a hole in the top and bottom of the cardboard "stage." Slip the dowel stick through (we used a 3/4 inch dowel from the craft store) so that the stage can rotate around the dictators.

When the dictator is facing the government building talk about the goals of that particular dictator. Then flip the stage around and talk about what actually happened in that country after the dictator took power. Do this a few times until your kids can recite or fill in the details with your help. We give some information below, but feel free to add to or substitute your own.

Joseph Stalin: He wanted everyone in Russia to be equal, so he controlled the entire economy as well as schools and churches. His economic policies resulted in mass starvation of some 6 million people. He also had a "Great Purge" to get rid of anyone who opposed him, and this killed another 1 million or so people from peasants up to the top army and political officials. The repression continued through his reign. Around 20 million people were killed by Stalin's government in all.

<u>Adolf Hitler</u>: He wanted to restore pride and honor to Germany and prove that Germans were the superior people on the planet, deserving to rule over everyone else. His regime killed about 5.5 million people in concentration camps, 19.3 million civilians and political prisoners, and also caused WWII, which killed another 29 million soldiers in Europe and around the world.

<u>Mao Zedong</u>: He believed that great people were not bound by moral codes but should strive for the "Greater Good." He thought the good thing for China would be to overthrow the government so that the working class people could be in charge. He wanted to take the wealth of the nation and give it out equally to all. In the "land reform campaign" around a million people were killed so the land could be redistributed "fairly." Mao set execution quotas which his willing soldiers happily exceeded. 4 to 6 million people were sent to forced labor camps so they could rethink their political positions. Most of these people died. 30 million people died of famine when the state forcibly took their grain production during the "Great Leap Forward." In all, between 40 and 70 million Chinese died in the implementation of Mao's policies.

<u>Fidel Castro</u>: He wanted people to be completely equal, so he controlled healthcare, education, and the economy. He imprisoned, enslaved, and killed thousands who disagreed with him, seeing them as enemies of Cuba since Fidel knew his way was the best way for Cuba. Thousands of Cubans fled his regime and immigrated to America or Latin American nations. Cuba became one of the most poverty-stricken places in Latin America. Cuba is still the most repressive state in the western hemisphere.

☺ ☻ EXPLORATION: Governments & Economies
Totalitarian governments are not new; they've been around under various names since government began in the unrecorded ages past. But the start of the twentieth century marked a time of a resurgence, a backlash against freedom. In the west, beginning with the United States, limited governments with constitutions had risen up with freedom and prosperity. People all over the world began to clamor for new government. In the aftermath of WWI, with the upheaval and hurts of that conflict, many fringe groups that desired power found they were able to seize it in the uncertain conditions after the war.

As a response to the freedom of the west, new political thought

Additional Layer
Often economics has more effect on government than anything else. If people are prosperous, they are happy. The reverse is also true. What were economic conditions like in each of the countries before totalitarianism began? Did things get better?

Famous Folks
Charles Lindberg was a 25-year-old U.S. Air Mail pilot in 1927 when he decided to attempt a record breaking flight across the Atlantic from New York to Paris. His plane was called the Spirit of St. Louis. Today it hangs in Washington D.C.'s Smithsonian Museum.

Read the *New York Times* headline announcing his great feat: http://www.nytimes.com/learning/general/onthisday/big/0521.html

On The Web

Watch this video about the Wiemar Republic and its comparison to 2010's United States: https://www.youtube.com/watch?v=GonYIEjVVWk

Additional Layer

In 1919 Attorney General A. Mitchell Palmer led a series of raids designed to root out communism. It was part of a larger movement called the Red Scare, which occurred in the years following WWI. The threat was not all imaginary. Dozens of letter bombs denouncing capitalism were mailed to the homes of law enforcement, politicians, and business leaders.

Additional Layer

The Great Steel Strike of 1919 was about technology taking the place of skilled steel workers. The steel workers wanted to ban the new tech so their jobs would be safe.

It, of course, did not work. But the history of that strike is important for more than the outcome or even the reasons. Find out what happened and how the various levels of government handled the strike. What do you think?

emerged and began to gain ascendancy over the ideas of liberty that had been given birth in the United States. Karl Marx was probably the most influential of the new thinkers. To learn more about him see Unit 4-4. Russia, China, North Korea, Japan, Argentina, Italy, Germany, much of Africa, the Middle East, and much of Central and South America adopted totalitarian communist, fascist, or socialist governments.

Government and economic systems are often confused with one another. There are three major types of government: anarchy, limited, and totalitarian. Associated with every government system is an economic system of one of two major types: free-market or controlled. In Unit 4-1 we talked more about these definitions, and you can find a printable to learn more here: http://www.layers-of-learning.com/government-types-for-kids/

Here: http://layers-of-learning.com/government-trivia/ you will find a government trivia game to print on card stock and cut out. Some of it is review from when you studied the United States government in Unit 4-1. Answers with explanations are on the cards. Play it once to learn and then again to test yourself.

☺ ☺ EXPLORATION: Russian Revolution

One of the most important events of the 20th century was the Russian Revolution. It affected not only Russia, but half of the world as Russia worked tirelessly to spread communism around the globe, reaching out to aching nations with money, guidance, and promises of prosperity and strength.

During World War I Russia was constantly short of food, lost major trade routes, and suffered horrible losses. People were very angry with the tsar. In order to finance the war, the government had begun to print money, resulting in inflation. The price of food quadrupled. But even though the price of food went up, the peasant farmers did not receive an increase in their income because the middlemen absorbed it all, still offering the old, low prices. The peasants, no longer able to afford the very food they were growing, stopped selling and reverted to subsistence farming, creating a major shortage of food in the cities. The inflation was affecting industry and wages of workers in much the same way, but they could not eat what they produced and many people began to starve to death.

Communist groups from the universities began to gain ground among the common people because of the harsh and difficult times. The tsar had many of the leaders exiled or thrown into Siberian prison camps, Vladimir Lenin and Josef Stalin being two of these. Back in 1903 the Communist Party had split into two groups, the more radical Bolsheviks, who were willing to use any means necessary to gain power, and the moderate Mensheviks, who thought murder was going too far.

In February and March of 1917 industrial workers in Petrograd (St. Petersburg) had gone on strike. Almost the entire city was shut down. People were marching and demonstrating all over the capital but most especially in front of the tsar's palace. Tsar Nicholas ordered his troops to put the rebellion down and end the strike by violence. The troops refused to fire on the crowd, which contained many women. With the loss of his troops, the tsar lost his government and was forced to abdicate.

An interim parliamentary government was set up, most of the officials being Menshevik Communists. Alexander Kerensky emerged as the leader of the government at this time. Even with a new leader, the problems that existed under the tsar had not magically gone away upon his abdication. Hunger, high prices and low wages, horrible defeats in the war, and political bickering continued. Kerensky tried to make changes and actually instituted more freedoms, but the people were still demonstrating. Ironically, it was Kerensky's opening up of political freedoms that invited Vladimir Lenin and his Bolsheviks in as a legally recognized political party. They saw the opening and made their bid for power.

The Bolsheviks worked hard all that spring and summer to stir up discontent. By October they marched with their Red Army, making war on the Provisional Government's White Army. The Bolsheviks won, and Lenin ruled with an iron fist, much more brutally than even the tsar. Millions more would die, mostly of starvation, but also by firing squad, torture, and prison work camps, all in order to create a "workers' paradise."

Vladimir Lenin stirring up support for his ideas in 1920.

Make a propaganda "piece" (poster, sculpture, short commercial, bumper sticker, slogan) that convinces people that you as dicta-

Additional Layer

In April of 1920 a cotton bubble destroyed the price of cotton for the next twenty years. Talk about economic bubbles and how they are caused.

This article explains the cotton collapse in detail: https://www.williamrawlings.com/images/Boll_Weevil-small_PDF_for_web.pdf

Additional Layer

Propaganda is biased or misleading information designed to persuade people to a certain political view.

This anti-capitalist poster is typical propaganda. It shows elites on top of the pyramid saying, "We rule you. We fool you. We shoot at you." The workers on the bottom are saying, "We work for all. We feed all." It tells a half-truth to create an emotional response in its viewers.

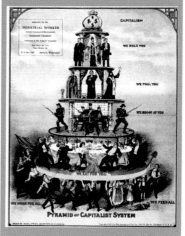

Writer's Workshop

Write a speech for an imaginary dictator to go with your propaganda piece.

Additional Layer

In 1922 Howard Carter and his team of archaeologists discovered the tomb of King Tut, reigniting Egypt fervor.

Additional Layer

In one example of how Hitler used industry as a tool of politics, he ordered the Volkswagen Company (a company founded by the German Labor Front in the first place) to build a car that everyday people could afford. The result was the Volkswagen Beetle. Hitler wasn't trying to be nice. He was using the car as a tool to gain more support by saying "Look, you can all afford a family car now, not just the rich." Hitler wanted the Germans to have as many cars as the Americans in order to prove that his government and his economic system were as good or even better.

tor of the world is the right move to make.

What lies do future dictators tell people to get into power? What slogans do they use? How can you see through it all to the truth of what they're offering?

☻☻ EXPLORATION: Weimar Republic

After World War I, governments like Germany, Austria, and Russia, that still had autocratic emperors, fell. Republics were very popular in Europe at the time, so nearly all the old empires became republics. The problem was that while the West had time to grow into their new freedoms and had time to economically and educationally advance, the East did not. Freedom was suddenly thrust upon them. Couple that with the aching recovery from World War I and none of these republics lasted for long.

The republic in Germany became known as the Weimar Republic after the city where the constitutional assembly convened. During the 1920s when Britain and the United States were experiencing such prosperity, Germany was in the depths of a terrible depression. They had lost many territories, including most of their agricultural land and all of their overseas colonies. They had to adopt a whole new currency, lost their pre-war export base, and were still blockaded by the allies who only allowed a few goods into Germany from the outside, most of which were far too expensive for average Germans.

But the worst of it was that the country was in massive debt from the Treaty of Versailles which demanded crippling war reparations payments (Germany finally made the last payment in 2010, and that's after a major debt restructuring and huge fine forgiveness). To pay for it, taxes had to be raised on an already impoverished and starving people. The German government could only raise taxes so much, so to pay off the debt they began to print money. Printing money led to inflation. Wages for the small percentage who actually had jobs could not possibly hope to keep up. Inflation turned into hyperinflation. The people were hopeless and broken. The republic that was supposed to bring them freedom and prosperity only brought more misery.

This is a book of million marks banknotes. To buy a notepad would cost billions of marks so people used the currency to write on instead.

They turned to a man named Adolf Hitler, who promised not only prosperity, but renewed hope and pride and strength. He promised to reunite Germany and rearm Germany. He also blamed the republican form of government and Jews for the troubles Germany had seen. In 1933 the German attempt at freedom was dead, and the Third Reich had risen.

For a great short history watch this: https://www.youtube.com/watch?v=0utEnQuIxsE

- What problems did the Weimar Republic have to overcome?
- What happens to a country when it incurs massive debt?
- What options does government have when faced with financial problems and unmet obligations?
- What did the Weimar Republic do to try to solve the debt problem? Did it work?

Now use the printable Weimar banknotes from the end of this unit. Cut the notes apart so you have four separate notes. Staple them together in a book. On the back of each note write down one fact about the Weimar Republic or about hyperinflation, what it is, how it is caused, and what it results in.

☺ ☺ **EXPLORATION: National Socialism**
Whatever alternative to the German government was offered, it had to be radically different from the Wiemar Republic and republics in general. It also had to promise jobs, food on the table, and some national pride. There were three contending political parties that tried to offer these things: communists, monarchists, and National Socialists, or Nazis.

Hitler was the head of the Nazi Party, which eventually came out on top. Hitler's government delivered all of the things the Germans wanted. He instituted a strong central government with one leader at the head, like Germans were used to. The money stabilized. The military was built back up, in violation of the Treaty of Versailles. Major works projects, like the Autobahn, were initiated by the government, which caused the unemployment rate

Additional Layer

The term "fascism" comes from the word "fasces," which is Latin for a bundle of rods tied around an ax.

The bundle of rods was a symbol handed to a Roman leader who had the power of corporal and capital punishment. The bundled rods symbolized strength through unity. The fascists often used this old Roman symbol for their own ends.

Additional Layer

Several states became fascist following the chaos and destruction of World War I. These included Italy, Germany, Yugoslavia, Greece, Lithuania, Poland, and Spain. Fascist coups were defeated in Hungary, Romania, France, Chile, and Brazil. Later, after World War II, Argentina became fascist. Today neo-fascist political groups and individuals still exist in spite of, or perhaps because of, the horrors demonstrated by such movements in the 20th century.

Additional Layer

In both Italy and Germany motherhood was celebrated. Women were given financial bounties for having large families. Women were discouraged and even barred from employment unless they were the only breadwinner in the family. The goal was a large population of children and youth to indoctrinate and raise as soldiers for the "Fatherland."

Governments have tried to control the family at different times and places in history. Can you think of some examples?

Fabulous Fact

The way Hitler talked up Germany as though it were superior to everybody else and so ought to rule everybody else is called Nationalism.

Writer's Workshop

Biographies are a great way to learn about historical time periods as well as individual lives. Write your own mini-biography of someone famous from this era. Use this printable notebooking page if you like http://layers-of-learning.com/printable-biography-notebooking-pages

to drop dramatically. And Hitler preached endlessly about how superior the German people were, which made people feel good.

To make all of these things happen Hitler had to silence the opposition. He created secret police (the SS), had his political opponents killed, and rounded up anybody who might oppose him, including communists, Jews, and foreigners. He got rid of anybody who might cast doubt on the perfection of his German race such as cripples, the mentally handicapped, or homosexuals. If you wanted to keep your job and avoid jail, you joined the Nazi Party. He took all industry under the wing of government and made it do what he wanted, including utilizing slave labor. Children were indoctrinated in the Nazi schools and taught to spy on their parents. There was no political, economic, or personal freedom in Germany, but there was food and greater prosperity than before.

Watch this short history of the Nazi rise to power: https://www.youtube.com/watch?v=vO-_HXO7HwY. It goes by pretty quickly, so you may want to watch it more than once.

Economically, Nazi Germany was a heavily controlled market. Politically, it was a brutal totalitarian regime. Most people describe it as fascist, but its results looked almost identical to the results of Russia under Lenin and Stalin: an outwardly prosperous and functioning society with an underlying fabric of slavery, abuse, murder, control, and international aggression.

At the end of this unit you will find a Nazi Germany notebooking page. Cut out the title and glue it to the top of another sheet of paper. Then cut out the Volkswagen Beetle shape. Cut along the dotted lines to create a flap where the door goes. Glue the Beetle, all but the flap, to the sheet of paper. On the outside of the car, write what the Nazis achieved for Germany. Inside the door flap, write how the Nazis maintained control of the German people so they could produce the results they wanted. Cut out the flaps for Adolf Hitler, Herman Goring, and Joseph Goebbels. Goring

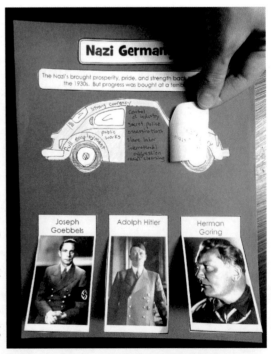

and Goebbels were two of Hitler's top cronies. Look up information on all three men and write facts underneath the flaps.

☺ ☻ EXPLORATION: Fascism & The Political Spectrum

Fascism uses the economy to further its goals of total domination over its people. The people are allowed to have no values or philosophies outside of the state mandated ones, including religion, education, or politics. Violence is seen as a proper method to achieve political dominance. Fascism is also extremely nationalistic, which is to say that its adherents believe they are superior to every other people on Earth, giving them the right and obligation to dominate everyone else. Fascists hate Marxists, capitalists, liberals, democratic liberals (conservatives in today's America) and anarchism, not to mention nearly everyone else.

Many people visualize a political spectrum where communism is on the far left and fascism is on the far right, with moderates smack in the middle.

In this view extreme political positions on either the liberal or conservative side lead to totalitarianism.

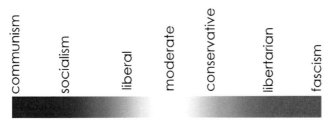

An expert on National Socialism, Roderick Stackelberg of Gonzaga University, said, "The more a person deems absolute equality among all people to be a desirable condition, the further left he or she will be on the ideological spectrum. The more a person considers inequality to be unavoidable or even desirable, the further to the right he or she will be."

- What do you think? Is this true?
- What are the implications of achieving total equality, and what are the implications of a forced inequality?

In Unit 4-1 we presented the political spectrum that the American Founders envisioned. The amount of government and personal liberty is significant rather than personal, economic, or political equality. Both communism and fascism would be on the far left of this scale.

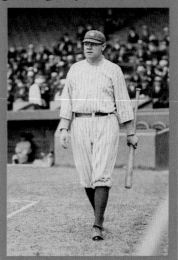

- Think about the differences between these views of government and society. Do you like one way of looking at the world better than the other?
- Are both views valid, only one valid, or are neither valid?
- Think about your own personal life. Are you personally concerned more with being equal to others or with having liberty? Is it necessary to chose between these two, or is it possible to have both?

Draw these two political spectra in your notebook. Explain in a few words what each represents. Beneath, write your ideas about the political spectrum and how you believe governments and political positions should be evaluated or compared. You can also create your own political spectrum diagram based on how you see government.

☺ ☺ EXPLORATION: Roaring Twenties

There was a little economic hiccup right after World War I and then a bigger, much more severe recession two years later in the United States. But factories retooled, new industries opened up, men found work, and business began to boom again. We call this eight year boom period during the 1920s, a time when the national wealth doubled, the Roaring Twenties.

One of the major changes that happened and that produced wealth during this time was that many factories retooled to make mechanized farm equipment. Mechanized farms meant that fewer people were needed to work on farms, freeing them to produce other things besides food. Millions from the countryside and from Europe poured into American cities looking for work in factories and offices. With a strong supply of labor, very low regulation, low taxes, and a highly educated workforce, American business boomed and the standard of living for millions increased dramatically, more dramatically than at any other time or among any other people in history up to that point.

Use the "movie reel" template from the end of this unit to show some features of the Roaring Twenties. Have the kids find aspects of the Roaring Twenties in your reading and draw one icon in each film square. For example, you could draw a Model T automobile, a Wall Street sign, a radio, a movie marquee, a flapper, a jazz instrument, a tall city skyline, or Babe Ruth. You can make a "screen" to show your movie on from a small box, like from gelatin dessert. Just cut a slit on the edges of one side, cut out a window from the front, and feed the paper through. We painted our box in silver to make a "Silver Screen."

☺ ☻ EXPLORATION: Prohibition

Prohibition was a ban (Constitutional Amendment 18) on the production, transport, and sale of all alcohol from 1920 to 1933. It happened because certain groups, such as the Women's Christian Temperance Union, lobbied and rallied for the ban of alcohol. They saw how the abuse of alcohol led to abuse of children and women, public disturbances, crime, idleness, and poor health. They thought if they could just make it illegal, then all these ills would disappear. The problems did not all disappear. The laws were ignored and people made and sold alcohol in secret.

The laws were repealed because the government lost much needed tax revenue during the Depression and because Prohibition led to a rise in organized crime in cities where crime bosses made big bucks off of the illegal alcohol trade. In short, because it couldn't be enforced, it actually spurred on more crime. John D. Rockefeller said this: *"When Prohibition was introduced, I hoped that it would be widely supported by public opinion and the day would soon come when the evil effects of alcohol would be recognized. I have slowly and reluctantly come to believe that this has not been the result. Instead, drinking has generally increased; the speakeasy has replaced the saloon; a vast army of lawbreakers have appeared; many of our best citizens have openly ignored Prohibition; respect for the law has been greatly lessened; and crime has increased to a level never seen before."*

The 21st Amendment repealed the 18th Amendment and ended Prohibition. It is the only constitutional amendment to repeal a prior amendment. Choose one or more of these activities to do as you learn about Prohibition:

Famous Folks

Charlie Chaplin grew up in horrible poverty in London. He began acting on the stage as a child with the help of his mother. He moved to Los Angeles in 1913 to work in the infant motion picture industry and became financially independent by age 26 as one of the most highly paid people in the world.

Famous Folks

Even though Prohibition was repealed, the United States still has laws on the books that limit the manufacture and sale of hard alcohol, or spirits. That's why we see so many microbreweries for beer and vineyards, but few start-up whiskey makers.

Fabulous Fact

A club that sold illegal alcohol was called a speakeasy. The name comes from the idea that you don't speak loudly about a bar that sells illegal alcohol.

- Watch this short introduction to Prohibition: https://www.youtube.com/watch?v=_CE4u6jI_rc
- Research more about Prohibition and make a list of unintended consequences to this law. Think about how a worthy goal: health, family peace, and public good, can be defeated if it is pursued in the wrong way. What basic Constitutional principles were ignored when all alcohol was banned?
- Compare Prohibition to the War on Drugs. Some people say drug use and distribution should be illegal because drug abuse is clearly harmful. Others argue that making drugs illegal just creates more crime. Should there be laws governing potentially harmful substances? What laws do we have now that govern drugs and alcohol?
- Explore this website's interactive map: http://www.pbs.org/kenburns/prohibition/prohibition-nationwide/#
- Make a label for a glass soda bottle using the printable from this unit. Record information about Prohibition on the label before attaching it to your bottle.

😊 😊 EXPLORATION: Immigration

During the first part of the 20th century, immigrants from southern and eastern Europe (mostly Italy, Greece, Poland, and Hungary) poured into the United States. In their home countries there weren't enough jobs because of improvements in mechanized farming. Some were also undergoing war and revolution. There was also a mass immigration from Norway and Sweden, which were united at that time and undergoing an economic depression as well as religious persecution. Most of the Norse ended up in the upper Midwest. Jews also flocked into the U.S., fleeing the pogroms of Russia and other hostile European states.

The United States was booming with industry, and everyone heard that you could get rich in America. In 1907 alone, 1.2 million immigrants became naturalized. Most of the new immigrants ended up in cities and went to work in factories. They provided the work force that catapulted the United States to the front of the industrialized nations.

So many immigrants were pouring in that some Americans became alarmed that they were losing their way of life. They feared that these immigrants would bring their lower standards of living, diseases, poor morals, bad genetics, and autocratic political views to their adopted country. Pressure was put on Congress and, in 1921, the Emergency Quota Act was passed, limiting the numbers of people that would be accepted from each country. The laws were tightened even further in 1924 and not relaxed until the 1960s with its Civil Rights movements.

Talk with your kids about how immigration has been both a blessing and problem for the United States or your own country. What are the good things about new immigrants? What are the challenges? Does your family have an immigrant past? Do you know the story?

Make a felt immigration story book. You'll need 8" x 10" sheets of craft felt, scissors, and hot glue.

Start by cutting out your immigrants. We used tan felt and a cookie cutter (intended for gingerbread men) to make our people. Then make clothes out of more felt pieces. Use hot glue to fix the clothes onto the people.

Make some backgrounds that you can use to tell the story of immigration. We made a boat and the United States with a few big cities. You could also make pages showing some of the countries your immigrants came from, pages showing the factories they worked in, or a page for the Ellis Island immigration station they went to for processing. Again, use hot glue to attach everything together.

Finally, assemble the pages into a book. Connect the pages by sewing them together or gluing them together.

Fabulous Fact

Fordney-McCumber Tarriff of 1922 is excellent for studying the effects of tariffs on trade between nations. It was designed to protect American farmers and American industry, but did it do that? What do you think?

Famous Folks

F. Scott Fitzgerald is a famous American author who wrote during the Roaring Twenties. His novel, *The Great Gatsby*, is especially iconic.

Fabulous Fact

The scare about immigrants was based partly in eugenics, a popular pseudo-scientific movement of the early 20th century. Eugenics pretended to be able to determine which genetic pool, from which races, was superior. Unsurprisingly, the race of the northern European proponents of the theory was found to be superior.

GEOGRAPHY: U.S. ECONOMICS

Teaching Tip

In the history sections of previous units we covered some of the major economic systems used throughout the world including capitalism, mercantilism, Marxism, and (in this unit) fascism.

If your kids are ten or older and you have not yet learned about these systems we recommend you begin there. You can get caught up by playing our Government Match Game: http://www.layers-of-learning.com/government-types-for-kids/

Additional Layer

Federal Reserve System, or Fed for short, is a central bank of the United States. They control all of the money for the whole country. If a normal bank wants more money to put into circulation they have to borrow it from the Fed and pay the Fed interest rates. In this way the Fed determines the interest rates for the whole country and can control important parts of the economy. They also supervise other banks and make sure they are safe places to put your money.

Economics is the management, distribution, and study of wealth. It may not seem to have much to do with geography, but money determines where people live, what they do, and relations between nations. Since geography is the study of current nations and peoples as well as the study of the land, we include economics in this unit. We will specifically relate money and wealth to the distribution and condition of people in the United States.

Today most people live in cities in the United States. Why? Why are the cities located in the places they are? As you proceed through this unit think about why people choose to live where they do. Why does your family live where you do? Did you live somewhere else in the past? Why did you live there, and why did you move? There are many reasons, but for most people at least some of the reasons have to do with economics.

☻ ☻ EXPEDITION: What Is Money?

We use money to pay for things we want or to get paid for work we do. Before money existed people had to trade, or barter, for things they wanted. Money makes it easier to trade because I don't have to hope I come across someone with something I want who also wants something I have. Instead I can just pay them money and then they can take that money and go buy what they want from someone else.

Money isn't really worth anything by itself. We only accept it in exchange for our work because we know that other people will accept it in exchange for their work. In fact, most money now is just numbers in a bank account, there aren't even actual pieces of paper or coins to represent all of the money we use.

The reason we want money is because without it we can't get the things we want and need. People give money in exchange for a place to live, food to eat, transportation, toys, clothes, vacations, and everything else. If you don't have money, it is very difficult to obtain those things.

But it is important to remember that money is not wealth. Wealth is the accumulation of things that have value, things that make our lives better. It could include land, a home, clean air, friendship, a pleasantly spent weekend, clothings, books, knowledge, or anything that makes you happy. Money is one important tool we use to pursue happiness; one of the foundational rights we recognize as Americans.

Money is controlled by governments. Only the money issued by the government will be accepted by someone who is selling something you want to buy.

Have your kids design their own paper dollar. Take it to a friendly store at a time when they are not busy. Have your child try to buy some small item with their homemade paper money (clue the cashier in ahead of time). Then give them actual U.S. currency to buy the item with.

Why does the cashier not want to take the paper money you made, but will take the paper money the government made? Everyone has agreed that the government money is worth something, but they have not agreed that your money is worth something. What do you think would happen if people decided the government money wasn't worth anything anymore?

☻ ☻ ☻ EXPLORATION: Government & the Economy

The economy is made up of all the financial transactions between people in the whole country. It includes buying and selling, working and earning, borrowing and trading.

Set up your own mini economy.

1. Invent your own money. Remember that money can be anything. Give it a cool name.

2. Have a parent be the government. The parent will also be a participant in the economy. The government can decide how much money it will allow in the economy. The government also has to resolve any disputes that come up and make rules about the money.

3. To start, the government should give out money in any way it likes, keeping back most of the supply. Allow borrowing, but

Additional Layer

The United States has a mostly market economy. In a true market economy the government would not interfere in the buying, distribution, or sale of goods except in the case of criminal activity or harm done. But the United States government does, in fact, heavily regulate economic activity.

Still, for the most part, people in the United States are free to make their own economic decisions without interference or force from government. Most people like that freedom, but more and more people are saying that sort of freedom leads to unacceptable inequalities. You should think about that as you learn more about how wealth is handled in the United States.

Additional Layer

In the United States the unit of currency is called the dollar. Other countries have other currencies. Mexico has the peso. Britain has the pound. Japan has the yen. If you go to a foreign country you have to use their currency. Banks can exchange currencies between countries.

Additional Layer

The government decides how much money is available and they control how much each dollar can purchase by altering the amount of money available. If there is less money, then each dollar is worth more. If there is more money, then each dollar can buy a little less. The United States government generally increases the money supply at a pretty quick rate which means that every year your dollar can buy less and less, or in other words, prices keep going up.

The increase in the money supply and resulting climb in prices is called inflation.

On the Web

Celebrity Calamity is a fun online game to play where kids manage a celebrity's finances for them. Kids have to collect money, buy only what is needed, decide whether to pay with credit or debit, decide how much to pay off on the credit card, and keep their celebrity happy by staying in the black. https://financialentertainment.org/celebritycalamity

charge for the service.

4. Make every interaction in your home a financial one. If a parent makes dinner, the eaters must pay for it. If the kids do dishes they get paid for their work. Individuals can decide how much they will charge and how much they are willing to pay.

5. At some point the government should flood the economy with money and then later severely restrict the supply. See what happens to prices.

6. The government should also put restrictions and rules on work from time to time as desired. For example, the government could require that people vacuuming the floor wear a dust mask which they must purchase. Or they could restrict work opportunities to only certain people or take money from some people to give it to others. If you have a very active and creative government you can even think of convoluted ways to tax people. Keep this up for as long as you like until the economic lessons are learned, and keep discussing as you go.

Make a point about how much the decisions of the government affect the economy and other aspects of how the economy worked. Talk about prices and how they were set. Did some people end up richer than others? Why?

☻ ☻ ☻ EXPLORATION: Wealth

Wealth is not exactly money, but money can be used as a measurement tool to tell us how wealthy someone is in terms of finances. To figure out financial wealth you add the person's total cash, bank accounts, mutual funds or stocks, and the worth of their home, land, businesses, and vehicles, plus other possessions. Then you subtract the debt that person has accrued.

You cannot tell how wealthy a person is by looking at them or their homes and cars. Someone with a very nice home, fancy cars, designer clothes, a top notch education, and expensive toys may actually have negative wealth if they have borrowed money to pay for all of those things. At the same time, someone with a small home, old cars, a blue collar career, and few toys might be very wealthy because they own their home and cars, have no credit card debt and a hefty savings account and investments.

Wealth is built through hard work and good financial decisions. Americans are some of the wealthiest people on Earth because we are hard-working and creative, and we have a free market economic system that allows us to keep the results of our hard work and creativity.

Additional Layer

If you have teens, check out these workshops from H&R Block. We especially like the one about credit cards.

http://www.hrblockdollarsandsense.com/what-were-doing/resources/

Teach your kids to build wealth by starting with a piggy bank. Collect three identical boxes or one long box with paper dividers. Let your children paint, cover with fabric, and embellish the boxes any way they like. Once the boxes are decorated, label one section "spending," one "savings," and one "giving." Decide on percentages of income that will go into each category. A good place to start is with the 70-20-10 rule. 70% of income goes toward spending. 20% of income goes toward savings. 10% of income is for giving to the needy, a charity, or as a tithe. The giving box should be emptied frequently, like once a month or so, so that the child gets in the habit of frequent giving. Also, it gets harder to give away money as the amount becomes larger.

A child's savings can be set aside for future education, buying a first home, or even to put in investments. The place they chose to put the savings should be a place that helps them toward future wealth. Savings is not intended to be spent on toys or other luxuries; that is just deferred spending. They can accrue money in their spending bank until they can afford the toy. Savings should be long-term and dedicated to more important ventures.

Coupled with this should be that income is based on work. Kids should be learning the lesson that money does not magically appear. They have to work for it. The amount of money they make for jobs should depend on your household income and how much money their labor is worth. At our house we all do regular chores without pay because we are part of a family, but we also offer special jobs for payment to give our kids practice with money.

Fabulous Facts

If you buy a candy bar, that means you cannot buy something else. That is opportunity cost.

Read *The Three Little Pigs* to learn about opportunity cost. Any version will do, but we like the true-to-original version by Paul Galdone.

The first two pigs skimped on work, building their houses so they could go out and play. What was the cost of their lost opportunity?

Guide your kids in applying this to their own lives.

Famous Folks

Too much debt is what killed the economy in 2008. People acted like they had more money than they really had. Then when they could no longer make the payments, it all came crashing down.

Additional Layer

If you have teens, talk through how interest payments work. Do some calculations. If you were to use the credit card to pay for your family purchase, how much extra would you end up paying in interest? How long would it take you to pay it off if you paid the minimum? This calculator can help: https://www.creditkarma.com/calculators/debtrepayment

Additional Layer

Of course, some people get into debt through no fault of their own. Prepare for the unexpected. Talk with your kids about emergency funds, when to use and not use them, and how much should be saved in them (about 6-12 months of living expenses). Discuss different types of insurance and what each is used for. Insurance, remember, is for financial security.

☻ ☻ ☻ **EXPLORATION: Debt**

The person with all the fancy stuff, as in the Wealth Exploration, usually looks like the happier person, but debt means that you owe someone else your labor. When you work and get paid, you have to pay your creditors first. If you don't, you will probably eventually lose everything you have, and people will stop letting you borrow. Debt is very stressful, especially when you begin to be unable to pay everyone you owe.

Debt is a huge problem among Americans. About 20% of Americans have no wealth or negative wealth because they are in debt. Around half of all Americans have credit card debt. Most of the time this is okay because people can still make the payments, and debt means more money is flowing in the economy overall. But if consumers become unable to repay their loans then economic catastrophe can befall the entire economy.

Remember that your most valuable asset is your labor and ingenuity. To trade away your future labor and ingenuity for cash in hand at the moment is a lot like the first two pigs in *The Three Little Pigs*. They wanted to play now, and so they suffered later.

Read the story of *The Three Little Pigs* to your kids. Talk about how the first two pigs chose to play instead of working to build something that would last. People who choose debt are usually choosing to play first and hoping that future work will pay for it.

Make a family piggy bank from a plastic jar, spray paint, a pipe cleaner, wiggly eyes, and felt. Label it with something your family would like to buy: a trampoline, a vacation to a National Park, a new television. Talk about how you could just use a credit card to go buy this thing, or you could save for it. Discuss which decision would be the wisest. Find out how much your purchase will cost. As a family, work to earn money to buy the thing you would like. Try to make this a long term project, but not too long.

Think months, rather than years. Every now and then, count the amount of money in the jar to see how close you are getting.

To make the bank, wash a plastic jar. Cut a slit in the side of the jar to slide money through. Make sure it is big enough for quarters and folded bills. Spray paint the jar and lid pink. Cut out pink felt ears and pink felt legs and glue them on with hot glue. Glue on wiggly eyes. Wrap a pipe cleaner around a pencil to make a curly tail. Glue the tail on with hot glue. Draw on a piggy nose.

☺ ☺ EXPLORATION: Supply and Demand

Supply and demand are the most fundamental principles of a market economy. Demand means how many widgets people want. Supply means how many widgets are produced. Supply and demand are related to price. If people demand more of a product, then the producers can charge more for it, and vice versa.

Watch this clip from *The Hudsucker Proxy* film: https://www.youtube.com/watch?v=Ng3XHPdexNM

Discuss the clip with your kids:

- Why did the store owner reduce the prices?
- Why did the store owner start raising prices again?
- What changed the prices?
- Who were the people in the office in shirts and ties? How is the neighborhood store related to corporations?

Now do some research on another product and its supply and demand changes. Here are some good ones to try out:

- Smartphones from 1999 to today
- Chocolate
- Arby's Brisket sandwich
- Tickle Me Elmo
- The Clapper
- Fast food industry

Create a poster on an 8" x 10" sheet of card stock that explains what you found. Include at least one graph (just a basic sketch; it doesn't have to be technical) of how the supply and demand increased and decreased over time.

☺ ☺ ☺ EXPLORATION: Marketing in Markets

When companies want to sell a product they have to let people know the product exists and create a desire in people to buy the product. This is called marketing.

There is no reason on earth why anyone would ever need a piece

---

Memorization Station

Memorize the definitions of these terms:
- market
- supply
- demand
- gross versus net
- goods
- services
- opportunity cost

Famous Folks

John Maynard Keynes, a British economist, had some ideas about how governments should cushion markets from high and low swings. The U.S. government uses a lot of his ideas today.

Another influential economist was Milton Friedman, an American who disagreed with the role of government in the economy. Compare them.

Writer's Workshop

Entrepreneurs are people who have ideas and start new businesses. They are the ones who grow the economy and innovate old fields or create new ones.

Write up an idea for a business you could start a venture in.

Additional Layer

Governments borrow money to pay for things just like individuals do. The amount of money the government owes is the national debt.

The government borrows money to pay for things like wars and welfare costs of all sorts. The government borrows money from individuals in the form of bonds and from other governments in the form of loans.

China and Japan hold more than a trillion each in U.S. debt. The U.S. debt is now larger than the entire GDP per year.

Just like individuals, government has to pay interest on its debts.

All of these debts and payments are the responsibility of the American people.

of pottery that could grow plants on its surface. And yet in the 1980s Americans began buying up Chia Pets by the thousands. The Chia Pet company had convinced people that parting with their hard earned cash in exchange for pottery that could grow sprouts would help them in their pursuit of happiness.

Watch a Chia Pet advertisement from 1990: https://www.youtube.com/watch?v=JIdYPrXmBAw

Every marketer follows four principles called the 4 Ps:

- Product: You must know your product and what makes it unique.

- Price: The price must be at a point where customers will pay for it and you will make the most money possible.

- Promotion: You must promote your product so that people will know about it and want to buy it.

- Place: People must be able to easily find and purchase your product.

How do the makers of the Chia Pets meet the 4 Ps?

Today an enormous amount of marketing is done on the internet. If you don't have a website, even if your product is not sold online, you're way behind the game.

Use the Marketing Worksheet from the printables at the end of this unit to investigate three American companies and their marketing. All three companies must be a part of the same market. For example, you could research three ice cream companies, three hamburger restaurants, three major league baseball teams, or three running shoe companies. You will go online and find their websites. Fill out the sheet comparing the marketing of the three companies. Some of this is your opinion, but as a consumer, all that matters is your opinion.

☻ ☻ ☻ EXPLORATION: Division of Labor

We often ask kids what they want to be when they grow up. This assumes that they have to choose some single thing to spend their lives producing. This assumption is part of free market philosophy. If each of us chooses to produce some small part of everything that mankind needs to pursue happiness, then we can all have more of that happiness (or at least the wealth that makes happiness possible). I can trade some of what I am producing for some of what you are producing, and we are both richer than we would be if we had not made the trade.

The further we specialize, the more we can produce, and as production increases, so does wealth. For example, when factories used specialization to take the place of craftsmen we had the Industrial Revolution, and wealth increased rapidly.

Do this exercise to show how specialization is useful. Have two or three groups (a group can be an individual) make all the same dish for lunch, each group making enough to feed everyone in the hopes of trading. Everyone makes macaroni & cheese; everyone makes peanut butter and jelly sandwiches, or everyone makes taco salad. Boring. Everyone still has what they started out with and no one is better off.

For dinner have each group specialize by each making a different dish for the dinner, enough for everyone. Now trade between groups. If group one made tomato soup then group two can trade some of its grilled cheese sandwiches for some of group one's tomato soup. Both groups are richer than they were before they traded.

☺ ☺ ☺ EXPLORATION: Scarcity

People are never satisfied. We always want more. But at any given moment there are only so many resources in existence. This idea that people always want more than they can have is called "scarcity" in the economic world.

Because of scarcity we have to make economic choices. Every time we make a choice we are deciding *not* to choose something else, which takes us back to opportunity cost.

At the end of this unit you will find a printable set of worksheets that will help kids plan a birthday party while staying within a budget that you set. We recommend a budget of about $250. Tell the kid whatever they don't spend on their party will be used to buy birthday presents. The first page is a bird's eye view of the room and yard where the party will be held. The second page has cut outs of things that could be added to the party. Each of the "party elements" comes with a price tag though. Let kids design their party any way they want. Once they have what they want and they've stayed in budget, have them glue the party into the birthday room.

☺ ☺ EXPLORATION: Gross Domestic Product

Gross domestic product is the total monetary value of all the goods and services produced within the country during a specific time period. The gross domestic product, or GDP, tells us how much the country is producing, and that tells us how healthy our economy is. If you have a high GDP, then the country is doing well. If

---

Deep Thoughts

A similar revolution in specialization is taking place today, but it is global specialization. You've probably noticed that if you call customer service you're most likely talking to someone with a thick accent, probably from India. That is because India has specialized into a customer service master. China is best at manufacturing simple goods. Japan is best at manufacturing technology. The United States is best at ideas. As countries specialize, wealth will boom.

Additional Layer

Here is an extreme example of scarcity from 1949 in Hawaii: http://the.honoluluadvertiser.com/specials/dockstrikes.html

What do you think of the dock workers striking? How did their decision create scarcity, and how did that affect the whole economy of Hawaii?

Fabulous Fact

Microeconomics is the study of financial decisions of individuals or single businesses. Macroeconomics is the study of the whole economy.

the GDP drops, then we might be having some financial difficulties as a nation. Another important number is the *real GDP*. The real GDP subtracts inflation from the total production.

You can use the GDP numbers to compare your country from year to year or to compare your country to other countries around the world. The countries with the highest GDP tend to also have the highest standard of living.

Go to http://www.bea.gov/national/index.htm#gdp and click on "Current Dollar and Real GDP." It is an Excel spreadsheet that you can open to see the history of the GDP in the United States since 1929, when they first started keeping track.

The "A" column of the spreadsheet shows the year. The "B" column shows the GDP in billions of today's dollars. Those are the only two columns you need to worry about. Examine the numbers. Do you see any times in American history when the GDP got smaller or stayed about the same? Are there times of especially large growth?

Take the last twenty years and graph them. How is the health of the United States' economy right now?

😊 😊 😃 **EXPLORATION: Caring For One Another**
Making and taking care of money is important, but it's only part of a healthy financial picture. A truly well-managed financial life also includes giving. Why? Because the better the world is, the better we are. Because the point of making money ought to be to increase well-being and happiness. When we are serving others cheerfully and willingly we are at our happiest. This is a fact of the human psyche, not a religious statement, though most religions have said something to that effect. Finally, if you can't part with your money willingly when there is nothing in it for you, then you are addicted to money. Being a miser never made anybody happy.

Read a book to your children about giving. We like *The Giving Tree* by Shel Silverstein and *The Quiltmaker's Gift* by Jeff Brumbeau.

Then make no-sew fleece blankets with your kids to donate to a hospital (for newborns or sick children), a police station (for kids in distress), or to a nursing home. Find a place that will welcome your donations before you start the project with your kids. For each blanket you need 2 yards of fleece for baby blankets, 3 yards for little kid blankets, and 4 yards for adult blankets.

1. Divide your fleece into two equal pieces. (You can use differ-

ent patterns/colors of fleece or the same for both sides). Lay them on top of one another, matching the sides. Then trim all the sides so it's nice and even.

2. Cut a 4" x 4" square out of each corner. Cut slits, 4" long and 1 1/4" wide, all the way around the blanket. The slits don't have to be perfect; just eyeball it.

3. Fold all of the strips up and cut a tiny slit on the fold of each strip, going through all layers of the fleece. Pull the end of each strip through the hole to make the "knot."

Make it a practice in your family to donate money, time, or service on a regular basis. Talk with your kids about why you give where you give and what good it does in the world. Here are some specific things you can do:

1. Donate money to your religious organization.
2. When you see someone in need, stop and help.
3. Go out of your way to say and do kind things for strangers.
4. Give money to a cause you believe in.
5. Spend time volunteering at a soup kitchen, a pet shelter, children's hospital, or a nursing home.
6. Regularly set aside a percentage of your family's income for charity.
7. Drop coins in the Salvation Army buckets at Christmastime.
8. Give to fundraisers.
9. Volunteer in a library, as a coach or tutor, or as a scout or 4-H leader.
10. When a disaster hits the world, give to the Red Cross or another aid organization.

Of course, all these things are far more impactful to your kids if they are directly involved.

On the Web

Inspire your kids with stories of other kids who have done amazing things to give. Here's one to watch together: https://www.youtube.com/watch?v=gg5l1u-E9Cs4

On the Web

You can find great charities online that can help your kids connect personally with people around the world who need help. Watsi is an excellent and transparent charity that helps people in poor places pay for medical bills: www.watsi.org

Always do your own research and make sure charities are really giving the money to people in need. Watsi gives 100%.

Writer's Workshop

Write a list of 25 random acts of kindness you can do. Include some that require money and some that just require time or talents. Commit to doing the things on your list, and as you do, write down some returns you've received as a result. Did you feel happy? Did someone do something good in turn? Did you improve yourself?

SCIENCE: VOLCANOES

On the Web

This 3 minute video is a good introduction to volcanoes for all ages: https://www.youtube.com/watch?v=WgktM-2luLok

Fabulous Fact

While melted rock is still under the surface we call it magma. Once it emerges we call it lava.

Additional Layer

Read more about one of these famous volcanic eruptions in history:

Thera c. 1500 B.C.

Mt. Vesuvius 79 A.D.

Mount Tambora 1815

Mauna Loa 1843-now

Krakatoa 1883

Mount Pelee 1902

Paracutin 1943

Mt. St. Helens 1980

Nevado del Ruiz 1985

Mount Pinatubo 1991

Eyjafjallajokull 2010

Mt. Pinatubo 1991

Volcanoes are the result of hot molten liquid under immense pressure under the crust of the earth. Most volcanoes occur along the edges of plates where pieces of crust are being forced under one another, creating extra amounts of molten material as the subducted plate melts under the surface.

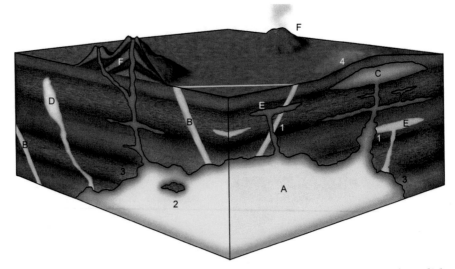

A: active magma chamber; B: old magmatic dikes; C: emerging laccolith; D: old pegmatite; E: magmatic sills; F: stratovolcano; 1: young magmatic intrusion cutting through an older one; 2: xenolith, solid rock transported from below or broken off the roof of the magma chamber; 3: contact metamorphism; 4: uplift at the surface

There isn't enough room under the crust, so the earth begins to bulge, eventually giving way in a magnificent pyrotechnic display of might. This type of volcano is called andesitic. It forms a steep sided cone and is found at plate margins. The thick lava produced is called andesite. Often the funnel of the volcano gets clogged with ash and cooling rock. An andesitic type of volcano can suddenly explode with little warning. Mt. St. Helens is an andesitic volcano.

This is Augustine Volcano in Alaska. It is an andesetic volcano.

This is a lava flow in Kilauea, Hawaii. It is a basaltic volcano.

There are other types of volcanoes called basaltic volcanoes. These form over hot spots under the earth's crust, usually in the ocean. These are places where the crust is thin and the magma is hotter. The magma wells up through cracks in the crust and slowly builds islands. Basaltic volcanoes are shield-shaped. The lava is thinner and runnier than andesitic volcano lava, so it runs further and faster. That's why the cone is lower and broader on basaltic volcanoes. The Hawaiian islands are basaltic.

☺ ☻ EXPERIMENT: Baking Soda & Vinegar Explosion

Ahh! The traditional baking soda and vinegar "eruption," which though certainly not a real eruption, is fun and memorable.

You'll need a glass or plastic bottle, vinegar, baking soda, dish soap, food coloring, and moon sand. Below you'll find a recipe to make your own moon sand.

Moon Sand
12 cups play sand (sold at home improvement stores)
6 cups corn starch
3 cups cold water

First, mix the corn starch and water thoroughly. Add the sand, a little at a time, until it is all mixed through. Store it in an airtight container. (You may need to add a tablespoon or two of water next time you play with it.)

1. Take your bottle outside and place it on a sturdy tray, like a baking sheet.
2. Pour 2 tablespoons of baking soda into your bottle. Use a funnel to make sure it all goes inside.
3. Now pile your moon sand around the bottle, making a nice volcano shape.
4. Mix a tablespoon of dish soap, 4 or 5 drops of red food coloring, and a tablespoon of vinegar in a large glass liquid measuring cup. Pour all at once into the glass bottle.

On the Web

Scholastic has a cool printable lift the flap book about volcanoes you can assemble. http://bit.ly/2jf622t

Additional Layer

This is a painting by Pompeo Batoni called Vulcan (c. 1700s).

It depicts the Roman God, Vulcan. Vulcan was the god of fire, and he gave his name to volcanoes. He was known as Hephaestus to the Greeks. Learn more about him.

Writer's Workshop

Obviously volcanoes can be very dangerous and destructive, but do they do anything good?

Find out and write about the good points of a volcano from the point of view of the volcano.

What would a volcano think of humans?

☺ ☺ ☺ EXPLORATION: Model Volcano

Make a model volcano out of salt dough. Model it in cross section so you can see the insides. Make sure your child can name all the parts of the volcano on the model.

1- inactive volcano; 2- fumarole; 3-secondary volcanic pipe; 4- volcanic pipe; 5- crater; 6- ash cloud; 7- volcanic bomb; 8-volcanic cone; 9- ash bed; 10-solid lava flow; 11- lava flow; 12- magmatic chamber

Salt Dough: (make one recipe for each child)

Combine 3/4 cups water, 2 cups flour, 1/2 cup salt, and 1 Tbsp. cooking oil. Mix together and add water until the dough just sticks together. If you put in too much water, just add a little more flour.

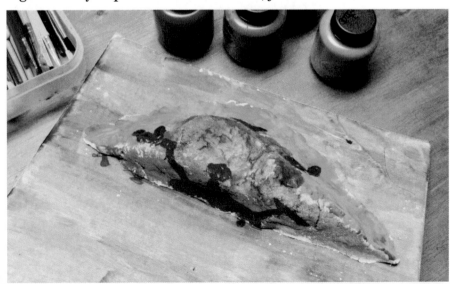

Shape it, then let it dry for a couple of days, or speed it along by putting it in a warm oven (200 degrees F) for an hour or so. After it's dry and cool you can paint it.

☺ ☺ ☻ EXPLORATION: Magma

Magma is thick, heavy, melted rock. It moves slowly, but it does move. It forces its way through pores in the rock, making the pores larger. The larger pores create cracks, which become rends. Eventually it forces its way up out of the surface.

Get a tube of toothpaste and poke hole or two in it. Leave the cap on and squeeze. The thick toothpaste squeezes through the little holes you left in the sides. This is similar to how magma moves through spaces in the rocks.

Now color the diagram of underground formations that happen as magma is squeezed through cracks and between layers of rock. See the printable at the end of this unit.

Here are the answers:

A. Magma chamber (batholith)
B. Dike
C. Laccolite
D. Pegmatite
E. Sill
F. Stratovolcano

1. New intrusion through old one
2. Xenolith (roof pendant)
3. Contact metamorphism
4. Uplift due to laccolith

You can also see the answers in the image at the beginning of this science section. Have your student look up what the words and processes mean.

Additional Layer

There are 16 volcanoes around the world that are classified as "Decade Volcanoes" because they are especially dangerous to human beings. These volcanoes are all pretty active and are located near large population centers.

They are called "decade volcanoes" because they were identified during the UN's International Decade for Natural Disaster Reduction in the 1990s.

Learn more about these volcanoes and where they are located. What makes them especially dangerous?

Mount Rainier in Washington is a decade volcano.

Additional Layer

Explosive volcanic events can affect people across the world. The ash and gases from a spewing volcano can block out sunlight and lower global temperatures. This famously happened in 1816, the Year Without a Summer. Find out more.

On the Web

This is a good six and a half minute video that gives plenty of facts, but is still understandable for even young kids. Use it before you play the "Escape the Volcano" game: https://www.youtube.com/watch?v=V863x-RoY2qk

Teaching Tip

The best time to read a volcano book to your kids is while they are working on a project. There's quite a bit of waiting for the pudding to cook, for example. So have a book handy.

Fabulous Fact

Not all volcanoes are mountains. They can be plateaus or just vents in the earth.

Lakagigar Fissure in Iceland is a crack in the earth that vented steam, gas, and lava for eight months in 1783-84. It killed most of the livestock and a quarter of the people in Iceland.

Photo by Chmee2/Valtameri, CC licnese, Wikimedia

☺ ☻ EXPLORATION: Escape the Volcano Game

Use this game to review facts after you have done some reading or watched videos about volcanoes. As you read and watch, have your kids take notes so that they can come up with questions to ask each other during the game.

1. Cut a box down so it has short sides. Spray paint the box in a background color (green or brown).
2. Find a small jar or container. We used a baby food jar. Build your volcano around the jar right on the box. We used an upside down paper bowl with the bottom cut out to add more volume to our volcano so we could get away with less dough.
3. Press tiny plastic or paper cups into the dough to make "spaces" on the game board. These will be the spots your pieces rest on as they play the game. Each player will have his or her own path down the mountain, so make as many paths as you have players. If you have more than four players, you'll want to play on teams or build a second volcano.
4. Paint the volcano any way you like; no need to wait for the dough to dry. We painted each of our paths down the mountain in a different color for each player and added a couple of painted on spaces to the flat area of the box. Each of our players made five steps to travel from the top to safety.
5. Let the paint dry, then add trees, rocks, moss, action figures, dinosaurs, or anything that makes it fun for your kids.
6. The little cups then become the pieces. You can draw faces on the cups and label them with players' names.
7. Pour vinegar into the container in the center of the volcano and add a teaspoon of baking soda to each player's cup.

<u>To Play</u>: Everyone starts at the top, in the space nearest the rim of the volcano. The first person asks the player on their left a question about volcanoes from the reading or video. A correct answer moves down the volcano toward safety. A wrong answer moves toward the volcano. Move around the table asking questions. If someone gets a question wrong and they are standing on the rim of the volcano, then they dump the contents of their cup into the volcano, and the volcano explodes. Play until everyone is either to safety or has made the volcano explode. Then you can refill your volcano with fresh vinegar and play again.

☺ ☻ EXPERIMENT: Mud Pots

Mud pots are boiling puddles or pools of mud, superheated by magma under the surface. Read about mud pots at the Yellowstone National Park website: https://www.nps.gov/yell/learn/nature/mudpots.htm. Click on the video link at the bottom of the page so your kids can see what the mud looks like in motion.

Mud pots are not directly heated by the magma. Magma close to the surface heats groundwater. The groundwater boils and steams underground, heating the earth above it. Surface water collected in puddles and pools is then heated indirectly by the groundwater. It's a lot like a double boiler in your kitchen.

Make a mud pot of your own with chocolate pudding.

Stir together in a glass mixing bowl (or if you own a double boiler, use that):

2/3 cup sugar
1/4 cup cocoa powder
1/2 cup corn starch
1/4 teaspoon salt

Gradually stir in 2 1/4 cups milk, whisking as you go.

Set a pot, half filled with water, on the stove. The stove is like the magma under the surface. The water is like the groundwater that is heated by the magma.

Set your bowl full of "mud" on top of the pot of water. Turn the heat on high. Do not stir. Keep cooking until the "mud" on top thickens with the heat. Ask the kids how the hot pudding is like a mud pot. Remove the pudding from the heat.

Stir in 2 tablespoons of butter and 1 teaspoon of vanilla extract. Spoon into individual dishes and cool in the refrigerator for two hours or more. Then you can eat it.

Additional Layer

Pele is the Hawaiian creator goddess of fire and volcanoes. It is said she lives in the crater of Kilauea, one of the world's most active volcanoes. Read more.

Sometimes lava from the volcano is blown by the wind and forms long strands called Pele's hair.

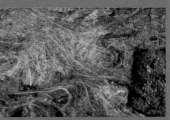

Other times it flies high in the air and cools before it hits, forming little tear-shaped glass stones called Pele's tears.

Additional Layer

The people of Indonesia throw offerings of flowers, money, and livestock into Mount Bromo once a year during the Yadnya Kasada Ceremony to appease the volcano and commemorate the first offering: a human sacrifice by ancient monarchs.

Fabulous Fact

Mud volcanoes aren't true volcanoes because they do not release ash or lava, but they are caused by tectonic activity beneath the surface of the earth. Hot water mixes with minerals and rock under the surface and boils up and out. There are around 1100 around the world on subduction zones.

This is a mud volcano in Taiwan.

Fabulous Fact

Not everyone buys into the mantle plume/hot spot hypothesis. Some volcanologists think that volcanoes in the middle of tectonic plates can be explained as places of stretching or thinning in the plate. In this hypothesis the mantle isn't any hotter in these places, it's just closer to the surface.

☺ ☺ ☺ EXPERIMENT: Hot Springs & Geysers

Sometimes the magma and heat from the interior of the earth is very close to the surface. Underground streams feed water into hot underground pools. If the path of the water to the surface is constricted through a narrow opening, then the heating water builds up pressure until the water erupts out as a geyser.

WARNING: Kids should stand back to prevent scalds from the hot water. Wear eye protection and heat protection for your hands.

You can make this happen in your kitchen. First, you need a tempered glass jar. The jar needs to be able to withstand direct heat, so a canning jar or a tempered chemistry flask are best. If you use a canning jar, you will need to punch a hole in the lid, big enough to insert a straw through. Besides the jar you need a straw, play dough or clay, a stove, water, and a saucepan.

1. Fill the bottle or flask 3/4 full with warm water.
2. Insert a straw, and stop up the edges around the straw at the neck of the bottle with clay or play dough. Make sure the straw is near the bottom of the bottle, but <u>not on</u> the bottom.
3. Heat directly on a stove top until the water in the bottle is hot enough to spurt out.

☺ ☺ EXPLORATION: Location of Volcanoes

Volcanoes erupt when rock from the mantle and crust melts. Rock melts whenever temperatures rise, pressure decreases, or water is added.

At convergent plate boundaries, places the plates are pushing against each other, the subducting plate gets heated as it descends and the plate melts. There is often water mixed with the sediments on top of the subducting plate. Subducting plates are oceanic plates, thinner and denser than continental plates. The water lowers the temperature at which rock must be at in order to melt, so it speeds up the melting as well. The Pacific Ocean is ringed with convergent plate boundaries, so there are hundreds of volcanoes all around the Pacific Rim.

Melting also occurs at divergent plate boundaries, places where the plates are spreading apart. When the plates spread apart there is space for mantle to well up. This decreases the pressure, making it easier for the mantle to melt. These types of volcanoes can be seen along the long trenches on the seafloor and in rifts in continental plates. Sometimes these volcanoes can grow high enough to form islands, like Iceland.

Most volcanoes are found at either convergent or divergent plate boundaries, but some are found in the middle of a plate. These are less understood. Many scientists think that directly underneath the volcano is a hot plume in the mantle, a place where the mantle is rising toward the surface. The hypothesis is that this movement decreases pressure and makes it easier for the rock to melt. There are about fifty different hot spots on Earth, mostly under the oceans. Hawaii, the Society Islands, and Yellowstone National Park are all sitting above hot spots.

Plot the locations of the volcanoes in the list below on a map of the world. Make a key for your map. Have a different color for each type of volcano: divergent plate boundary, convergent plate boundary, or hot spot. Look up information about the volcanoes to determine which type of volcano each is. Be able to explain why the conditions at the volcano's location make it so eruptable. (Hint: In the lists below, the first list is of volcanoes over hot spots, the second is of volcanoes on convergent boundaries and the third is of volcanoes on divergent, or rift, boundaries.)

Mauna Loa	Mt. Fuji	Eyjafjallajökull
Kilauea	Mt. St. Helens	Azores
Easter Island	Mt. Pelee	Dallol Volcano
Yellowstone	Mount Akutan	Kilimanjaro
Galapagos Islands	Mt. Vesuvius	Ascension Island
Piton de la Fournaise	Paracutin	Mt. Nyiragongo
Mt. Cameroon	Mt. Tambora	Udokan Plateau

☺ ☺ ☻ EXPERIMENT: Effusive vs. Explosive

There are two main types of eruptions: effusive and explosive. Effusive eruptions occur when magma wells out of the ground somewhat slowly and flows across the surface. Mauna Loa in Hawaii has effusive eruptions. Explosive eruptions are sudden and violent, with huge plumes of ash and lava spewing high into the air and zooming mud flows racing down the sides of the mountain. Mt. St. Helens in Washington State had an explosive eruption.

An effusive eruption happens when the magma chamber is made up of mafic magma. Mafic magma is less viscous; it flows easily,

Fabulous Fact

Remember back to when we were learning about felsic and mafic rocks in Unit 3-11? Felsic magma, the thicker kind, becomes granite rock. It usually cools beneath the surface of the ground because it is too thick to squirt out. Mafic magma usually becomes basalt and it most often cools above the surface because it's runnier and gets squirted right out between the rocks.

Additional Layer

There was a group of artists who painted the volcanoes of Hawaii in the 1880s and 1890s. They are called the Volcano School. Look up some of their art.

Kilauea, 1890, Eduardo Lefebvre Scovell

Volcano at Night, 1885, Jules Tavernier

Many other artists have painted volcanoes. Check out Andy Warhol's Volcano or Turner's volcano.

so it comes out of the ground fairly easily. Less pressure builds before it is released. Watch this video of an effusive eruption in Hawaii: https://www.youtube.com/watch?v=3Bm1L3iGnEU

An explosive eruption happens when the magma chamber is filled with felsic magma. Felsic magma is viscous; it is thick, so it does not flow very easily. This means it has to build up a lot of pressure before it is released. When a felsic volcano blows its top, it is dramatic. Watch a video of an explosive eruption in Indonesia here: https://www.youtube.com/watch?v=CsAo5jdCjoM

Make four packages of gelatin dessert according to the package directions, but using half the normal amount of water. Pour the gelatin into a gallon zipper bag and set in the fridge to cool for 3-4 hours. Cut a few little slits in the zipper bag and apply pressure to the bag. The gelatin is pretty viscous, but it will still flow out of the cracks. The earth has cracks in the crust like your bag does and the pressure that builds beneath the surface makes the magma squeeze out and flow down. Press too hard though and it could get explosive!

☻ ☻ ☻ EXPLORATION: Volcano Types

Mafic eruptions tend to produce broad, gently sloped volcanoes. They can be massive though, like Mauna Loa in Hawaii, the largest mountain on earth. These are called shield volcanoes.

Felsic eruptions tend to produce taller, steeply sloped, cone shaped volcanoes like Mt. Fuji in Japan. These are called composite volcanoes.

Cinder cone volcanoes are the last type. They are smaller, but with steeply sloped sides. They are usually formed from a single eruption and found near or on the slopes of a larger volcano.

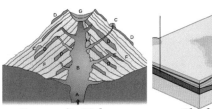 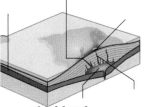 

Composite Volcano   *Shield Volcano*   *Cinder Cone Volcano*

Draw a diagram of each type of volcano on a sheet of paper to put in your notebook. Why would mafic magma form shield volcanoes and felsic lava form composite volcanoes?

☺ ☺ ☻ EXPERIMENT: Magma and Oobleck

Magma is a non-Newtonian substance. Under high pressure it's solid, but as the pressure is relaxed it turns to liquid. Magma is held together by interlocking chains made of silicone bonds.

Make some Oobleck to feel what the texture of magma might be like under the surface of the earth. When you press it, it feels solid, but when you relax the pressure, it runs easily, like a liquid.

1 cup water   2 cups corn starch   orange or red food coloring

Just mix the three ingredients up in a bowl. It works best if you put the food coloring into the water before you begin mixing.

☺ ☻ EXPLORATION: Types of Volcanic Eruptions

Besides being classified as either effusive or explosive, volcanoes can be further defined into categories. Here are six types of eruptions from the least violent to the most violent: Hawaiian, Strombolian, Vulcanian, Surtseyan, Pelean, Plinian.

Use the info from Wikipedia: https://en.wikipedia.org/wiki/Types_of_volcanic_eruptions to learn more about each type of eruption.

On a long sheet of freezer paper paint six volcanoes in a row. The first should be shield shaped and the rest cones. Paint what each type of eruption looks like.

THE ARTS: ABSTRACT ART

Explanation

As we enter the realm of the more modern art movements we can't show as many paintings because the artists' works are still under copyright. Make the effort to look in galleries, or at least in art anthologies or on the internet to see and familiarize yourself with lots of abstract paintings.

Teaching Tip

Just as your kids' version of Van Gogh or Michelangelo won't have the skill of the artist's genuine paintings, they likely won't be as skilled as the modern artists who used abstraction either.

We have kids make art in the style of the masters to help them remember and recognize the great art, not to try to exactly duplicate it. During this unit, you might want to point out the complexity of art, whether its realistic or abstract, and discuss the many years artists put into their training to develop whatever style they choose to paint in. Most famous artists spend the majority of their lives developing their skills.

Abstract art does not attempt to be an accurate depiction of anything in the real world. It is the opposite of realism, the aim of which was to make paintings look as true to life as possible. It has no recognizable subjects. Abstract art uses colors, lines, shapes, and forms to create pictures that stand on their own. To some, they don't look like anything, but then again, that's the idea: a painting doesn't have to "look like" anything to be enjoyed or to have value. Abstract art is creativity and imagination on a canvas. It inspires curiosity.

The Expressionist painters were the first ones to really delve into a lot of abstract art. Abstract expressionism began around the time of the World Wars in the early 1900s. Since that time, much of the art of the 20th and 21st centuries has been created abstractly.

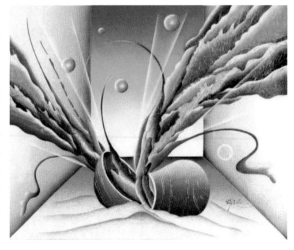

Often abstract artists play with and rearrange colors, lines, and shapes as they create. They add many layers and interesting details to their paintings. A lot of the art from this style is playful.

Most abstract artists don't have one particular meaning behind their art, but rather, they want the viewer to bring his or her experiences to the piece and interpret their own meaning. It is the combination of the expressiveness of the painter and the experiences of the viewer that combine to create the overall feeling and message of an abstract painting.

Some people ask, "Is abstract art really even art?" If art's purposes are to inspire, teach, make us question, and cause us to think, then certainly abstract art achieves all of that. A painting does not have to be realistic to serve a purpose any more than a story is only worthwhile if it is true.

☺ ☻ EXPLANATION: How To Evaluate Abstract Art

Because abstract art isn't meant to be realistic, sometimes we aren't sure what to look for in it. A lot of people claim that it just looks like a kid did it or that abstract artists don't have real talent. There are some real skills involved in abstract art though. As you look at paintings from this period, consider these things:

- Complexity - Look at the paintings on this page alone. We can ask kids to make reproductions of them, or similar paintings, but they won't actually have the complexity of the paintings of mature artists.
- Color - Color theory is an important part of art. Colors must be coupled in either cohesive or striking ways.
- Texture - One of the ways that abstract artists achieve texture is by layering. The paintings are made layer by layer, with each one adding new textures.
- Composition - Balance and focal points are important to paintings, whether they are realistic or abstract. Great art has components that draw our eye, beginning with the focal point and then traveling around the painting with strategically placed objects.
- Meaning - Even abstract art is planned out and intentional. When we look at great art it has meaning and makes us think about or feel something. Often the longer we look at it, the more meaning it has to us.

☺ ☻ ☻ EXPLORATION: The Pioneer of Abstraction

We talked about Wassily Kandinsky in Unit 4-8, for he was one of the great Expressionists. As his career progressed, he ventured more and more into abstract expressionism, or paintings that were full of feeling and color, but without realistic subjects. Sometimes abstract art is called "non-representational," because the picture doesn't look like, or represent, any real object.

You can make your own Kandinsky-style art using circles and squares. Get some colorful chalk. You can create this on black card stock or go outside on a concrete surface with sidewalk chalk. Begin by drawing a grid of twelve squares. You might want to use a ruler or yard stick to get straight lines (although even Kandinsky's squares were not perfectly straight). Use various colors of

Famous Folks

J.M.W. Turner created landscapes with elements of abstraction long before Kandinsky. In many of his later paintings his focus was on light rather than realism.

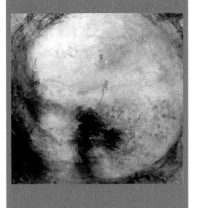

Expedition

One great difficulty of learning about art in books is not seeing it in person. Standing in a gallery and looking at an original painting is quite different than viewing the same painting online or in a book. Images lose their texture and depth, and in that loss, I've found that they also lose some of their meaning. Whenever possible, take the opportunity to view original paintings.

Layers, textures, and depth are an extremely important part of abstract art. If possible, go on an expedition to a museum near you to see for yourself.

Additional Layer

Stretch wide rubber bands across a 6" white tile. Use as few or as many as you would like in your own pattern.

Once they are all in place, apply a quick, thin layer of spray paint to the tile. You can use one color, two colors, or several.

Once it's dry, remove the rubber bands to reveal your own interesting line art.

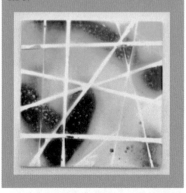

chalk to draw concentric circles in many colors inside each box. The circles do not have to be perfect. Completely fill the boxes with color. If you get the chalk wet before you draw it will be more vivid.

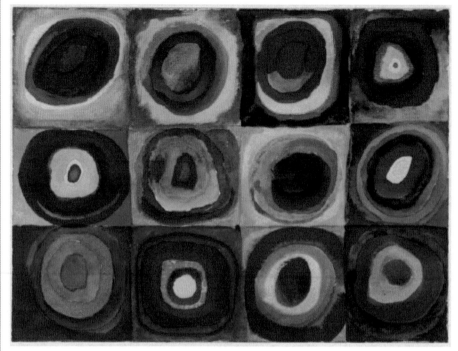

☺ ☺ ☺ EXPLORATION:Piet Mondrian

Piet Mondrian grew up in Holland. After he finished regular school he studied to be an artist. He painted things you see every day in Holland. But then he traveled to Paris. In Paris he decided he didn't want to paint everyday things anymore; he wanted to make neat designs with simple lines, shapes, and colors. He carefully placed squares and rectangles on his canvas, working to make designs that felt just right, with good balance and perfect harmony between colors and lines. His most famous paintings were made with geometry and primary colors, with grids filled in using color blocks of red, yellow, and blue, along with black and white. Here are two of his color blocked compositions:

Use a ruler to create your own grid lines in your sketchbook. Mondrian painted his grids in a variety of styles and sizes, so don't feel limited as you make your own grid design. Use red, yellow, blue, black, and white paint to fill in your grid and make a Mondrian-style abstract.

☺ ☻ ☻ EXPLORATION: Picasso's Cubism

Cubism was an art movement during the early 20th century. Painters decided to make one picture from several perspectives. They used a lot of geometric shapes, visible planes, and a fractured, disjointed style. Pablo Picasso invented the Cubist style. He is one of the most famous painters of all time, in part, because of his radical new ideas in painting. Go visit this website which includes a short video biography of his life: http://www.biography.com/people/pablo-picasso-9440021

You can make your own art based on some of the principles of cubism. Draw simple overlapping geometric shapes in your sketchbook. Try to create some overlapping intersections, meaning, have some lines and curves of your shapes land on the lines of other shapes. For example, one side of a triangle could also be made into the side of a parallelogram, have a smaller rectangle using one its sides, and also have the curve of a circle sitting on its edge. Fill your page with many overlapping shapes and lines. You can turn the page all different directions as you are working to see your picture from new perspectives. Cubism allows you the freedom to change spatial planes and perspectives as you go.

Now fill in your shape with a variety of patterns and colors using oil pastels. Again, feel free to turn your page in any direction as you work. There is no top nor bottom. After you are finished coloring, add thick outlines using black tempera paint where your pencil lines were. Can you spot a heart shape in the picture above? How many triangles do you see? Can you find a parallelogram (hint: one of its short sides is touching the bottom of the heart)? Just like the shapes in this picture are broken down, Cubist painters divided their subjects into parts.

On the Web

Here's an online art lesson about Picasso for kids. It lasts about 15 minutes and looks at some of Picasso's art, then makes a Cubist style dog portrait. Get out your supplies and paint along with her.

https://youtu.be/slYX-1OUKuhI

Additional Layer

Spontaneity was an important part of painting for many of the early abstractionists. Like the Impressionist painters, the process of making paintings was as important as the appearance of the finished paintings. Many abstract artists moved around their art studios, examining things from various angles, and some even moved while applying paint to the canvas. Have you ever done anything spontaneous? Is spontaneity a good trait?

Famous Folks

Georges Braque painted with Pablo Picasso and helped him create and refine the ideas within the Cubism movement.

Along with painting, he made many famous collages, called papier collés (French for "paper collages"). He even turned his paintings into collages by adding bits and pieces of newspapers and advertisements on to his canvases. He also used stenciling.

Because of his groundbreaking ideas, he helped usher in pop art, which used some of those same techniques.

Besides collages, he also made many still life paintings, but his work tended to stay in the realm of abstraction. Even when Picasso abandoned Cubism for other styles, Braque kept using the style.

☻ ☻ ☻ EXPLORATION: Picasso's Faces

Because Picasso liked to draw things from different angles on a single painting, sometimes the faces he painted looked really funny. Use a plastic mask from a craft store to make your own interesting face. Down the center of the face, lightly sketch a profile version of a face, the outline as though you are looking at someone from the side. Use a pencil and draw lightly so you can make adjustments as needed. On the other side of the face, fill in facial features as though you are looking at the person straight on. Fill in each side of the face and the features with brightly colored paints, using two contrasting colors for each side of the face. Try your mask on.

☻ EXPLORATION: Gravity Paintings

Gather craft pom-poms, wooden clothespins, large paper, a drop cloth or plastic tablecloth, and a paint tray filled with many colors of paint. Clip several pom poms to the wooden clothespins. Place your paper on the floor on top of the drop cloth. Holding it by the clothespin, dip a pom pom into paint, getting it thoroughly coated. Stand up above your paper and unclip the clothespin, allowing the paint-filled pom-pom to fall and leave

a mark on the paper. Repeat over and over, adding lots of color to your gravity painting. Experiment with dropping them from different heights, some just inches above your paper and some from higher. You can even stand up on a step ladder or chair to get extra high.

Afterwards, have a discussion about the experience.

- Did the pom poms always drop where you wanted them to?
- Did you think about where the marks would be when you dropped your pom poms?
- What created your painting - you or gravity?
- Could you create these same marks by painting them with a paintbrush in the traditional way?
- Abstract artists often use the process of making their painting to help communicate an idea. An artist who made a gravity painting might want to communicate how uncertain life is, or how we aren't always in control of our destiny, or that even good intentions can make a mess. Can you see a relationship between any of those ideas and your gravity art?
- Did you make a picture of anything? Do you think it means anything?

☺ ☺ ☺ EXPLORATION: 5 Minute Flip The Canvas

Sit in a spot that inspires you. It could be your bedroom, your favorite park, a spot in the city, or any place you really love. Start a five minute timer, and then begin to draw or paint something you see. When the five minutes is over, reset the timer and flip your page 90 degrees. Begin painting another element of the scene. Continue doing this every five minutes until you feel your picture is complete.

☺ ☺ ☺ EXPLORATION: Painting the Music

One of the things abstract artists are applauded for is their ability to create rhythm in their paintings. That is a really hard concept to grasp. What is the difference between a painting that has rhythm and one that does not? Often rhythm is created by repeated shapes and patterns. Artists repeat elements in their work with just the right amount of variation to keep things interesting. They also paint with a flow of continuous movements and strokes.

After you've discussed these ideas, get out your painting supplies and turn on some music. Sometimes it helps to actually paint along to music as you try to create rhythm. Choose a song you enjoy listening to and paint along with the rhythms in the song. Match your brush strokes, color choices, and designs to the music. Do you feel your painting fits the mood and rhythm of the song?

Additional Layer

The popular story goes that Isaac Newton was sitting underneath an apple tree when an apple fell on his head, and that is what gave him ideas about gravity. If the story is true, there is likely a great deal more to it than that, especially considering how brilliant his related scientific insights were. Not just anyone would extend a falling apple to an understanding of the moon's orbit.

This tree, known as Newton's Tree, is supposedly a descendant of the famous apple tree that sparked Newton's revelation.

Make a list of other things that you could use in a gravity painting besides pom-poms. Would anything on your list make an interesting shape when dipped in paint and dropped on to your page?

Writer's Workshop

Can you think of other ways you can paint using action? Write a story about a man named Arty who goes about his day adding to a painting he is making with each new thing that happens to him.

Start with the line, "Arty never went anywhere without his paintbrushes..."

Deep Thoughts

Read what some of these artists thought about abstract art. What do you think?

"There is no abstract art. You must always start with something. Afterward, you can remove all traces of reality."

-Pablo Picasso

"The more horrifying the world becomes, the more art becomes abstract."

-Ellen Key

"All art is abstract, because art is an abstraction of the truth."

-Milford Zornes

"Abstract art is not the creation of another reality, but the true vision of reality."

-Piet Mondrian

☺ ☺ ☻ EXPLORATION: Action Jackson

Jackson Pollock was an artist who was known more for how he painted than for his actual paintings. He made action paintings. He put large pieces of unstretched canvas down on the ground, then moved to and fro with cans of paint and brushes, splattering and dripping paint as he went.

Watch this Khan Academy video that showcases Pollock's action painting style: https://youtu.be/NToSHjOowLA

Make your own action painting. Break about a dozen eggs carefully, preserving the halves of each shell in an egg carton. Add a variety of colors of washable liquid tempera paint to each egg shell half. Go outside and set up a piece of foam board in an area that can get messy (rain will wash the paint splatters away if you use washable paint). Throw the eggs at your foam board canvas to create your own action painting.

☺ ☺ EXPLORATION: Scratchboards

Layering was an important technique of many of the abstract artists. They painted layer upon layer, adding to their paintings over time. You can make your own scratch art to see how to create a neat effect using layering.

First, use oil pastels to make a design of your choice on a 4" x 6" piece of card stock. For layer #2 you will draw with a white oil pastel on top of your colors, swirling and combining the colors below together. Layer #3 involves painting over the whole thing with black tempera paint. You will likely need to add several layers of the black paint. Paint on a thin layer. Let it dry completely before adding another layer. Continue the process until the paint is completely covering your design. Let it dry really well.

You will then scratch off part of the paint layer to reveal bright colors underneath. Use something metal that has a pointed tip, like tweezers or a fork, to scratch off the areas where you want to reveal color.

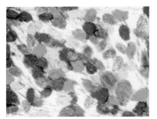  

☺ ☺ **EXPLORATION: Drop and Swirl**

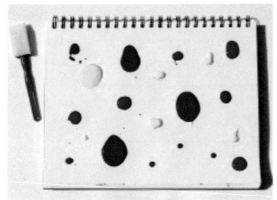

Make your own abstract painting in your sketchbook. Gather colors of paint that you like and drop blobs of paint right on your page. Make some of the drops large and some small. Spread them out all over your page.

Use a sponge brush to begin swirling the paint blobs around, creating colorful abstract swirls. Remember that the lighter colors will be completely covered because of color mixing if you aren't careful. Fill your whole page with the swirling colors.

Famous Folks

Karel Appel was a Dutch painter, poet, and sculptor. He is known for his childish and spontaneous paintings. He traveled all over the world, earning international recognition for his unique style.

Image courtesy of Karel Appel and the CODA Museum under CC by SA 3.0.

Coming up next . . .

Unit 4-10

Great Depression
Heartland
Mountain Building
Kinds of Art

My ideas for this unit:

Title: _____ **Topic:** _____

_____
_____
_____
_____
_____
_____
_____
_____
_____
_____

Title: _____ **Topic:** _____

_____
_____
_____
_____
_____
_____
_____
_____
_____
_____

Title: _____ **Topic:** _____

_____
_____
_____
_____
_____
_____
_____
_____
_____

Title: _____ **Topic:** _____

_____
_____
_____
_____
_____
_____
_____
_____
_____
_____
_____

Title: _____ **Topic:** _____

_____
_____
_____
_____
_____
_____
_____
_____
_____
_____
_____

Title: _____ **Topic:** _____

_____
_____
_____
_____
_____
_____
_____
_____
_____
_____
_____

Bolshevik Revolution

These are workers from Russia who are angry because they can't make enough money to feed their children or pay their rent. There is no way to get an education or better their lives. They see the greed of the rich nobles and factory owners and know those people will hold on to their power no matter what. They decide their only hope is to overthrow the government, with violence if necessary. This is how totalitarian regimes often begin.

Unit 4-9 Timeline: Totalitarianism

Oct 1917 4-9 Bolshevik Revolution in Russia 	**1920 4-9** Bolsheviks have solidified their power and Russia is renamed Union of Soviet Socialist Republics (USSR) 	**1920 4-9** More Americans now live in towns and cities than on farms 	**Aug 1918-4-9 Mar 1919** Post-war recession in the U.S.A. 
Jan 1920-4-9 July 1921 Severe recession hits the U.S.A./Europe 	**Nov 1920 4-9** Warren G. Harding wins presidency by a landslide 	**1920-1933 4-9** Prohibition on alcohol in the United States 	**1923 4-9** German hyperinflation 
Jan 1924 4-9 Vladimir Lenin dies, Joseph Stalin takes over 	**Aug 1923 4-9** Harding dies in office, is succeeded by Calvin Coolidge 	**Aug 1928 4-9** Kellogg-Briand Pact "outlaws" war. 	**Nov 1928 4-9** Herbert Hoover wins presidency 

Totalitarian Dictators

Joseph Stalin

Adolf Hitler

Mao Zedong

Fidel Castro

Nazi Germany

The Nazis brought prosperity, pride, and strength back to Germany in the 1930s. But progress was bought at a terrible price.

Joseph Goebbels

Adolph Hitler

Hermann Goring

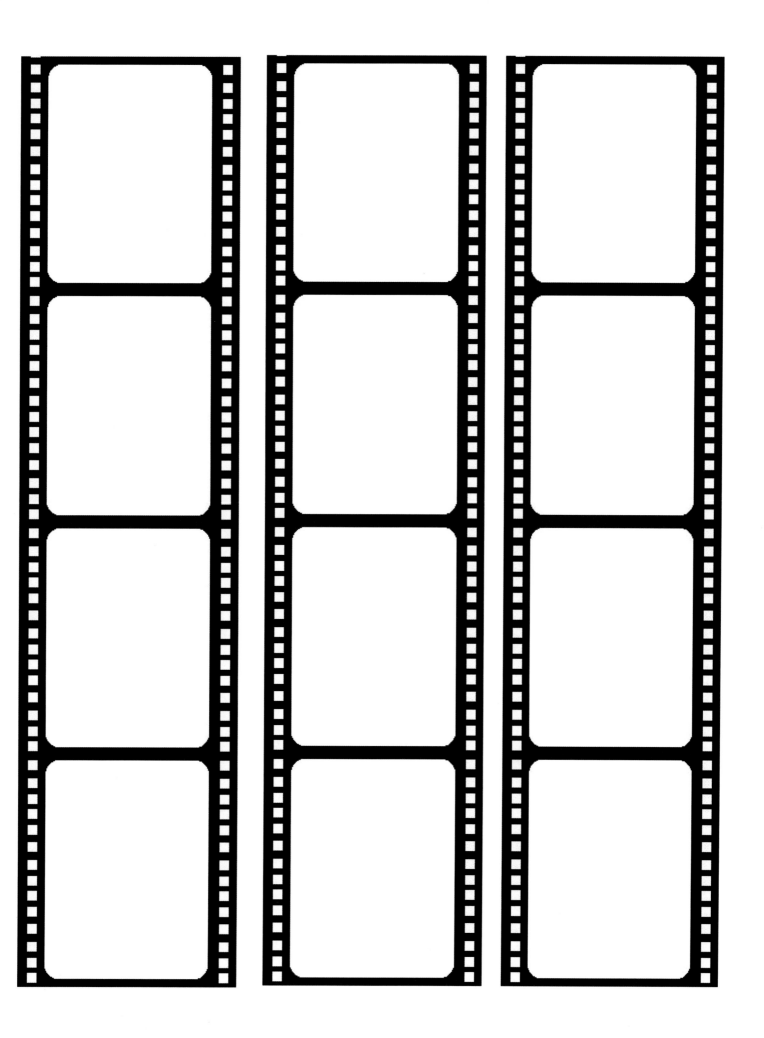

Prohibition Bottle Label

Cut out the bottle label and fill in your answers. Attach the label to a straight sided glass bottle to help you remember what Prohibition was about and what happened as a result of it.

What happened after the 18th Constitutional Amendment passed?

Why were women's groups for Prohibition?

What was Prohibition?

Marketing Worksheet

	Company 1	Company 2	Company 3
Product: Describe the packaging for the product and how much you like it compared to the others.			
Product: How many varieties are offered?			
Product: What is the slogan, and how does this appeal to you?			
Place: Where can you buy this product? How accessible is it to you?			
Price: How much does this company charge? How does that compare to the others?			
Promotion: Does the company have special offers or coupons?			
Promotion: Which website appeals most to you?			
Promotion: Where does this company advertise? TV, You Tube, social media, print, radio?			

Plan Your Party!

Put everything in to your party that you want without spending more than _____.

Party balloons $10

Bouncy Castle $160

Cake & ice cream $25

Water gun fight $10

Donut on a string game $5

Clown $200

Decorations $30

Goodie bags $50

Hot dogs & soda $15

Homemade obstacle course $0

Homemade water blob $20

Pin the tail on the donkey $5

Pizza & soda $50

Roller skate party $250

Twister $20

Inflatable water slide $150

Volcanic Structures

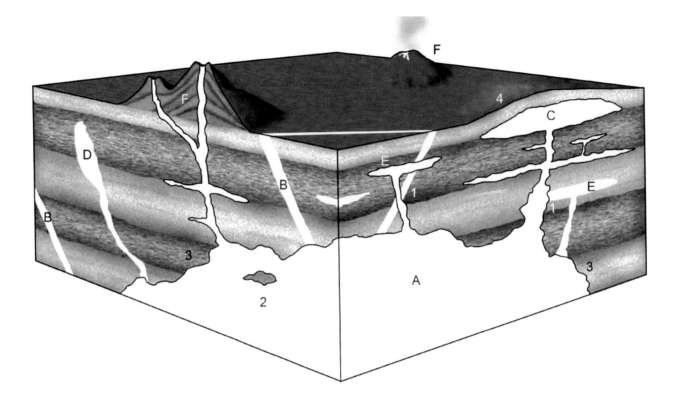

Structures A-F	Processes 1-4
dike sill laccolith magma chamber (batholith) pegmatite stratovolcano	contact metamorphism new intrusion through old one uplift due to laccolith xenolith (roof pendant)

A. _____

B. _____

C. _____

D. _____

E. _____

F. _____

1. _____

2. _____

3. _____

4. _____

About the Authors

Karen & Michelle . . .
Mothers, sisters, teachers, women who are passionate
about educating kids.
We are dedicated to lifelong learning.

Karen, a mother of four, who has homeschooled her kids for more than eight years with her husband, Bob, has a bachelor's degree in child development with an emphasis in education. She lives in Idaho, gardens, teaches piano, and plays an excruciating number of board games with her kids. Karen is our resident arts expert and English guru {most necessary as Michelle regularly and carelessly mangles the English language and occasionally steps over the bounds of polite society}.

Michelle and her husband, Cameron, have homeschooled their six boys for more than a decade. Michelle earned a bachelors in biology, making her the resident science expert, though she is mocked by her friends for being the Botanist with the Black Thumb of Death. She also is the go-to for history and government. She believes in staying up late, hot chocolate, and a no whining policy. We both pitch in on geography, in case you were wondering.

Visit our constantly updated blog for tons of free ideas,
free printables, and more cool stuff for sale:
www.Layers-of-Learning.com

Made in the USA
Middletown, DE
04 April 2025

73769535R00038